A FIGHT FOR LIFE

ONE WOMAN'S STRUGGLE THROUGH THE
SECOND WORLD WAR TO A NEW LIFE IN CORNWALL

The Moving Story of Gisela Hawkey
written by Ingo Küster

A Fight for Life
One Woman's Struggle through the Second World War to a New Life in Cornwall

The Moving Story of Gisela Hawkey
written by Ingo Küster

© P&B Hawkey 2016

Published in 2016
by P&B Hawkey

Translated from German by Hayley Johns

A catalogue card for this book is available from the British Library.

Paperback ISBN: 978-0-9956383-0-3
Ebook ISBN: 978-0-9956383-1-0

Publication managed by TJ INK
www.tjink.co.uk

Printed and bound by TJ International, Cornwall, UK

In loving memory of my family who died together on May 1st 1945.

My Grandmother, Martha

My Father, Friedrich and Mother Klara.

My sister, Helga and brothers Klaus and Peter.

Contents

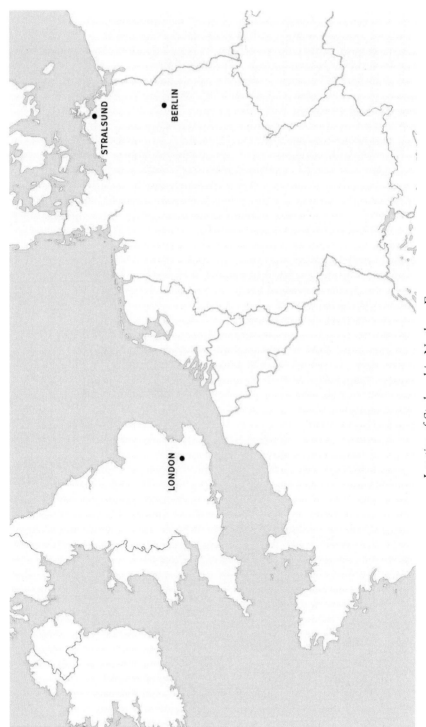

Location of Stralsund in Northern Europe.
© OpenStreetMap contributors.

Germany Today.
© OpenStreetMap contributors. By Permission Digitaldruck Kruse, Stralsund.

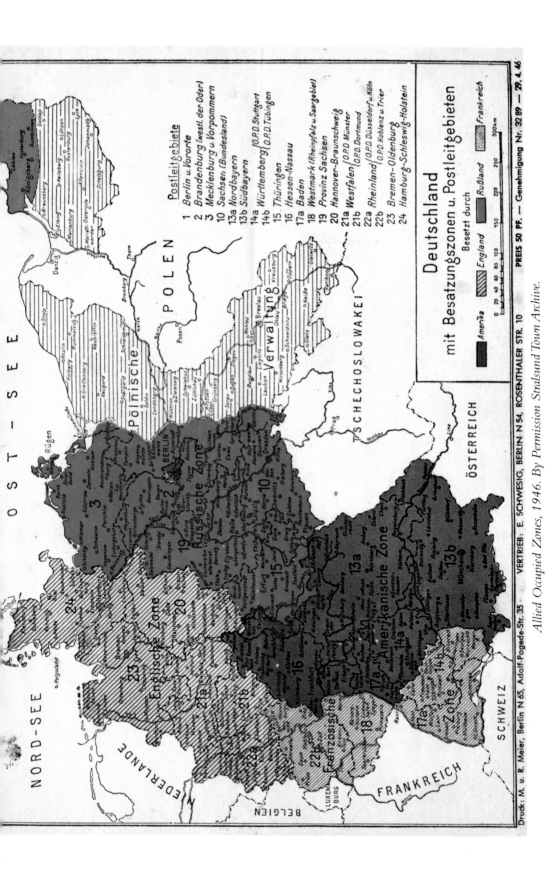

Allied Occupied Zones, 1946. By Permission Stralsund Town Archive.

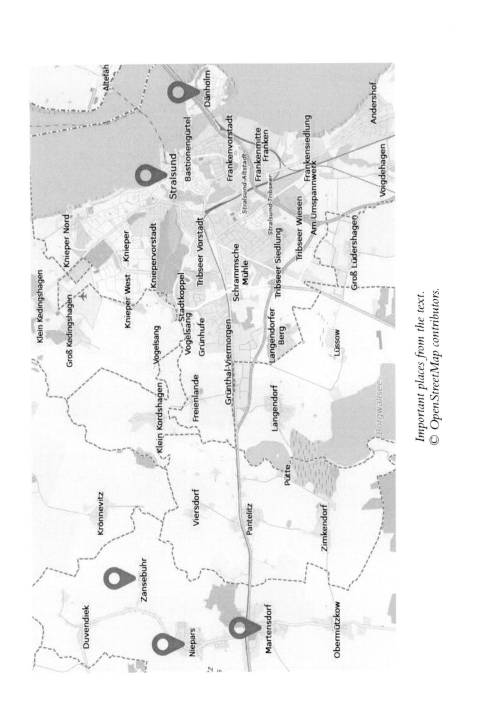

Important places from the text.
© *OpenStreetMap contributors.*

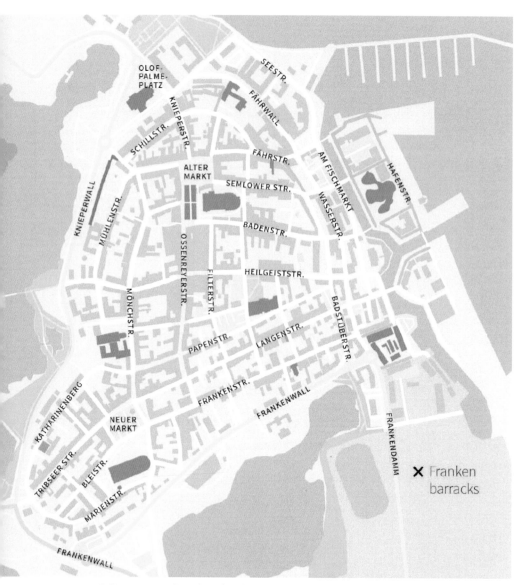

A Street Map of Stralsund Today. The Old Barracks marked with an 'X'.
© *OpenStreetMap contributors. By Permission Digitaldruck Kruse, Stralsund.*

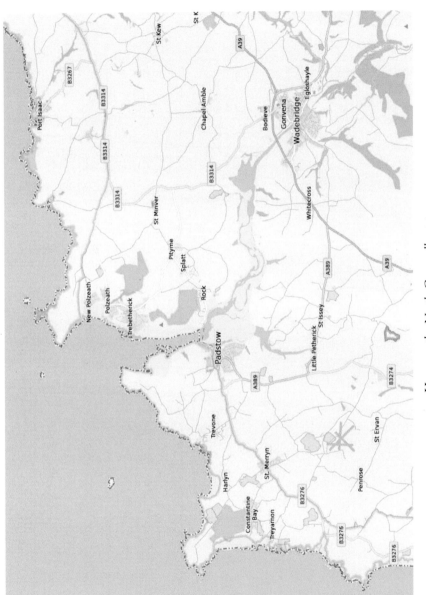

Home on the North Cornwall coast
© *OpenStreetMap contributors.*

Acknowledgements

For many years friends and family have told me my life should be written down. On one hand it is only a small tale of one life amongst millions. But it does also provide an individual perspective of an important time in social history. To those who encouraged the creation of this book here it is. To other readers, I hope you find it engaging and interesting.

First and foremost I must acknowledge the work of my godson Ingo Küster. Without his energy and enthusiasm this book would not have been written. I am so grateful to him for making it happen.

I thank my two sons, Peter and Bruce, for their work in liaising with Ingo and bringing to fruition an English version of Ingo's original German text.

Grateful thanks to Hayley Johns Translation Services (info@hayleyjohns.com) for her professional, timely and sensitive approach to translating this work. Also to Digitaldruck Kruse (www.mv-druck.de/wir-sind-bald-wieder-online/) and TJ INK & TJ International (www.tjink.co.uk and www.tjinternational. ltd.uk) for their professional help in bringing this book to print in Germany and the UK respectively. Thanks also to Clemens Photography in Bodmin (www.clemenscameras.co.uk) for their work in scanning and bringing old photographs and documents to life and to Drew Frisby for proof reading and writing a foreword. I am also thankful to The Stralsund Town Archive (www.stralsund. de) for use of images and maps and to Adrian Langdon (www. adrianlangdon.com) for his photographs of Wadebridge.

My life has had its share of desperation and pain alongside much happier times. It is impossible for me to list all those who have played an important part in 'seeing me through' the dark times, and as the saying goes, 'made life worth living' in the good times. If I tried to do such a list I would forget some who should be included and that would not be fair. Despite some very hard times so many people have shown me love and kindness in my life I cannot record you all, but you are all immensely valued.

I will mention:
Hamilton Hawkey, my husband. Words cannot express…
Peter and Bruce, my sons and the joy of my life.
Dr Temo Melikidse, Tbilisi. He saved my life.
Ingo Küster for making this book possible.

Gisela Hawkey.

Ingo Küster with Gisela Hawkey (née Schönow).

Foreword

Gisela's story is a fascinating one, its narrative full of proud highs and tragic lows, chronicling events that could easily be mistaken for fiction. When she first claims to have lived an eventful life, one could brush the expression aside as preamble, but it is truly an understatement, for she has lived through the darkest days of Nazism, the Second World War, and the subsequent occupation of East Germany by the Soviet powers, not to mention the continued tragedies that have plagued her journey to build a new life here in Cornwall.

When her sons, Peter and Bruce, first asked me to read their mother's life-story, I approached the work as something of an intellectual curiosity – an opportunity to flex my editorial muscles and perhaps learn more about a period of history I have already spent a good deal of time studying – but I had not prepared myself for the rawness of her story, or indeed its enduring relevance. I came away imagining the novels that might be spun from the various episodes and 'what-if' moments in the text, but it should not be forgotten that these events truly happened; like much of the very best fiction, this story is about the extraordinary experiences of an ordinary person. It is sometimes said that the purpose of fiction is to view life through a different lens, that we might shed some light upon our own lives by imagining those of others, to give ourselves the benefit of perspective – Gisela's story is a reminder that we do not always need to look to fiction to find stories that, particularly for those of us who have not experienced conflict in our lives, can offer a lens unimaginably different to our own.

This story is both sobering and reflective, but it is also a tale of resilience, courage, and faith, from which great inspiration can be taken. Gisela could easily have taken her story to the grave, without ever telling it in its entirety – as, regrettably, so many others of her generation already have – but luckily for us she has chosen to preserve it in this text. Her story should be of interest to anyone, both as a remembrance of darker times and as a reminder that even the greatest hardships can be overcome.

DH Frisby, Alma mater, Bath Spa University.

Gisela at age 91.
Permission of Owen Morgan.

Introduction

I have lived an eventful life, and now that I've reached a ripe old age, I notice that those closest to me — whether they are the same age as me or younger — are starting to leave this world. They leave gaps behind them, and leave too the certainty that the time we have left will only grow shorter. I've often spoken to my two sons about how I ought to tell my story, to write it up; it is a link between the extraordinary things that have happened to me and the social conditions of my time, and how these conditions developed subsequently into the international power struggle of the twentieth century.

There are many reasons for not doing so before now. Sometimes I hesitated, and sometimes there were not enough hours in the day. Now, though, I've decided at last that I must tell it. And perhaps it will do me good, to think that I shall leave it behind me.

This story spans a good ninety years, and begins at a time in which, in Germany, national and international conflicts were beginning to escalate, bringing closer nothing but a ruinous fate. It encompasses the Second World War, the Cold War and its boundary between east and west, and the end of this division through Europe. Many times, because of what I have lived through, I had reason to rail against my fate, to doubt the meaning of life. On occasion, I may even have lost the will to live. But in the end, an inherent force helped me to go on — it helped me to demand everything I could from life.

Gisela Hawkey.

The Early Years

The first of my parents' children, I came into the world on 14th July 1924 in the small German village of Niepars, near Stralsund, in a region on the Baltic now split between Germany and Poland. We later became a family of six, my parents' happy and healthy marriage having produced another three younger children: my sister and two brothers. At first, we lived at my maternal grandparents' house; in the right-hand side they kept a grocer's shop, while the other side served as living quarters for all eight of us. Living close to nature as I did in my childhood in Niepars is something I have held dear my whole life – even today, when I look out over my green and blooming garden, it delights both my heart and my senses.

My parents' wedding party outside my grandparents' house, 1923.

My grandparents' business must have been successful, for we never wanted for anything at all. At the time of their marriage in 1923, my parents were still very young; my father was twenty-seven years old, and my mother just twenty-one. Even as a young man, though, my father had served in the German Imperial Navy, surviving the

Battle of Jutland in 1916. I remember him telling me that he had trained as an engineer, and had even won an Iron Cross – that has always stuck in my mind – He was later captured along with his 'U' boat 157 and spent a long time as a prisoner of war in Norway.

My father Friedrich Schönow in his Imperial Navy uniform, complete with Iron Cross, 1st Class and sub-mariners insignia

Though my mother trained in business, she never worked in that field as, once her children were born, she devoted herself completely to caring for her family. That included, though, spending a short while as the owner of a small farmstead in Zansebuhr, a small neighbouring village. My grandparents financed the farmstead as a way of securing their daughter's livelihood. So I remember it all vividly, because as a child I was often allowed to romp around the farmyard and play in the hayrick. Likewise I spent a great deal of time with horses – a passion which I continued to cherish in later years.

My mother Klara Schönow, née Schmidt.

In the Hayrick with Mum and Dad.

Something I remember very clearly, and which still pleases me to think of, is my parents' happiness and their love of life. They were both good dancers, and would go out dancing whenever they could. In their wonderful attitude, they gave their children a piece of advice for life.

My Childhood

The land where I grew up is a flat plain as far as the eye can see. Only now and then do forests or gentle hills interrupt the sweeping vista. In winter in particular, when nature throws off its green cloak and the cold air reigns, you can really take in the vast expanse of the landscape. The Baltic Sea is close by, meaning that the climate is sometimes harsh and stormy, although the temperatures in summer as in winter do not rise or fall to quite the extremes that they do further inland. Periods of stable weather over days and weeks prevailed across all four seasons. I can remember many times, as a child, winter temperatures of -20 degrees Celsius, cold enough for the shallow lagoon (known as the Strela Sund) to freeze, allowing us to skate to the island of Rügen.

From a distance, you can see Stralsund's mighty church spires, connecting you to the town from afar. When I lived in Zansebuhr there was, and still is, a railway station in the neighbouring village of Martensdorf. This is on the mainline from Rostock to Stralsund. From here, we could get to Stralsund relatively easily, as it was only two stops away. The connection was often used by all those who lived in the area, whether it was for school, for work, to visit officials or offices, or simply to go shopping. Only very few families had cars at that time, and we were not one of them.

This part of Pomerania on the Baltic has a particularly beautiful coast: wide beaches with fine white sand, pine forests, and islands nestling close to the shore, inviting us to visit. Between these islands and the mainland are relatively small, shallow lagoons, called *Bodden* in the local dialect. Beyond the islands lies the open sea. In spring and autumn, thousands of cranes populate the ploughed fields and shallow waters, and in summer people take their place on the coast. Later, when I lived in Stralsund, I often swam with my family or friends in the sea.

My birthplace, then, was in Niepars, in my grandparents' house. My memories are full of beautiful, happy pictures – my parents managed to make a happy home for me and my siblings, Helga, Peter and Klaus, who were four, eight, and fourteen years younger than me respectively. By modern standards, life was really very simple. We played, for example, with stones, sticks, or just a ball. We sang children's songs or had stories read to us. Both parents had prepared us for a life according to the ideas of the day, and made every effort for us. Our requirements for a happy life were very simple, and were based on mutual devotion and empathy, but also on being able to cope with problems, big and small, independently.

Klassenfoto II 1932 mit Lehrer Voß

1. Reihe, oben links: 3. Erich Braun, 10. Zell
2. 4. Irmgard Warkenthin, 5. Walli Krause, 6. Traute Schönberger, 7. Hanni Martens, 8. Waltraut Lehnert, 9. Erika Schelhase, 10. Gertrud Happe.
3. 1. Emma Bräsel, 2. Irmgard Krüger, 3. Ilse Böst, 4. Grete Dähn, 5. Herta Schult, 6. Elli Hübner, 7. Käthe Hermann, 8. Hannelore Guhde, 9. Irmgard Liedtke, 10. Grete Harder, 12. Friedchen Harke, 13. Lilli Redmann.
4. 1. Annemarie Jonas, 2. Gertrud Pawlowski, 3. Käthe Heitmann, 4. Ursula Drews, 5. Margot Gellin, 7. Hildegard Liedtke, 8. Anneliese Meier, 10. Gerda Dewald, 11. Elli Braun, 12. Irene Möller, 13. Gisela Schönow.
Untere Reihe: 1. Alfred Herter, 4. Gerhard Jonas.

My School Class in Niepars. I am No 13 in Row 4.

My parents' work on their farm had brought me much closer to nature. Day after day, we were occupied with the cattle and with working the fields, and my parents had to work hard to be able to harvest enough. We children had plenty of opportunities to play outside in the yard or in the garden, and we made friends with the neighbouring children.

But education was not far away. At first, I went to the village school in Niepars, and later to the secondary school at Frankenwall in Stralsund. Each year, more and more of us children from the village travelled every day by train to school in Stralsund – we called ourselves the *Fahrschüler*, the travelling pupils. From this small group, I made friends with whom I managed to stay in touch, or who I encountered years later in one way or another. Each morning we walked – and later cycled – in all weathers over three miles to the station in Martensdorf, and every afternoon we came back again the same way. Only in the winter did families try to house their children with relatives in Stralsund. I went to stay with my Aunt Lotte and Uncle Wilhelm, whose two children were a similar age to me. Their flat was small, but that didn't worry me. If a harsh frost had formed, we would make our way to school over the frozen ponds, which we children of course loved to skate over. A game I especially liked to play was 'Name the Countries'; Fritz and Hanni – my two cousins – and I would open the atlas and, while one of us said a country or city, the other two would have to look for it on the map. It was a very exciting game to us, and we later remembered it very fondly. My knowledge of geography at school improved as a result, too.

On my parents' farm in Zansebuhr, with my sister Helga and my brother Peter

Schoolwork came easily to me. Aside from my mother tongue, in the upper school I studied two more languages, namely English and French. Naturally, at the time I had no idea how this would later help me.

By the time my family moved to Stralsund, my childhood was practically over; and so began a new chapter in my life.

7

At Home in Stralsund

In 1936, when I was twelve years old, my father took up a job with the navy in Stralsund. As he had served with them in the First World War, he was already familiar with them, and so he knew exactly what he was letting himself in for. Being an engineer by training, he was in charge of the repair and maintenance of the technical services for the barracks where the navy lived, which were just south of Stralsund's old town, only a few minutes' walk from the harbour. He was responsible too for the barracks on the island of Dänholm, as well as at Sassnitz-Dwasieden on Rügen (Germany's largest island).

A silhouette of the Stralsund skyline from the water. It looks now just as it did when I lived there.

Our first home in Stralsund was on Semlower Strasse in the old town, bought by my parents with the proceeds from selling the farm in Zansebuhr. For my father, it was not difficult to leave behind this rural way of life – as a trained navy engineer, he hadn't felt an affinity for it. The job in Stralsund was much more appealing to him. At the time, during the Third Reich, there was incidentally a period of economic boom in Germany, and in this respect the country was very optimistic – I could sense it too. My family then consisted of five of us; my younger sister Helga and brother Peter had been born and brought up in the countryside. They, of course, moved with us to our new home in the town, and my maternal grandmother lived then in Stralsund as well, at the St. Jürgen-am-Strand convent. My grandfather, though, had died in Niepars before we moved, and was buried in the churchyard there.

Urban life in Stralsund was a welcome change for me. As a child, I was always very curious – I still am today – so I was pleased that there was lots to discover and explore in Stralsund – not to mention that our journey to school was shorter, so I had much more time to do my homework and to play games and sports with my friends. In Niepars, I had been a member of the German Gymnastic Federation, and in Stralsund I practised my gymnastics more and more.

My father and my younger brother Peter on Stralsund's Heilgeist Strasse.

My parents were evangelical Christians, so we children were raised in the same faith. I had my confirmation lessons with Father

Hemmelgarn, a navy priest – the commandant's daughter was in my class too. At Christmas, our whole family would go to a service at the Nikolai Kirche (Church of St Nicholas); the whole church was beautifully decorated for the festive season, full of the blue uniforms of the navy. It was an unforgettable experience.

After some time – it must have been in 1937 or so – my father's new job in Stralsund meant that we had to move into the service accommodation within the navy's barracks. The flat was in the so-called 'Falkland Block' over the medical center, in the middle of the barracks on the Frankendamm. My parents sold our old house on Semlower Strasse – which later turned out to be a stroke of luck. A year after we moved into the new flat, my younger brother was born; his name was Klaus, though we all knew him as Klausi. Although we had moved twice in quick succession, life in our family carried on much as it had done before.

Living inside the barracks meant that we always needed a certain document to go in and out past the sentry, who stood on guard duty at the entrance. I can remember quite clearly how, once we had shown the permit, the watchmen would salute and let us pass. At first, I was very impressed by all this, but I soon got used to it. It wasn't just the watchmen on duty at the barracks' entrance, but sailors, officers, and petty officers too, who we would meet every day in the courtyard on their exercises. In spite of these surroundings, though, I felt safe and, by the time I had grown into a young woman, I only ever heard one wolf whistle.

Until I left school at the age of sixteen, I was also a member of the Hitler Youth. Under Nazi rule, it was expected and accepted that most young people would join its ranks – because we were convinced by propaganda and bound together by our collective naivety, as I later had to admit. Nevertheless, we had some excellent outings with the Hitler Youth to Hamburg: Schleswig-Holstein, and even to the Black Forest, which, quite apart from any political background, I very much enjoyed. These were often walking holidays where we stayed in Youth Hostels. In fact, I think these trips helped me to mature and develop as I grew up. When the regime was brought down, though, we didn't speak about any of that any more.

My pass for the Franken barracks as an assistant with the Red Cross.

The onset of war in 1939 did not seem to affect us at all. We all pursued our familiar tasks and duties, whether that meant at school, at work, or at home in one way or another. We worked on our allotment, went on daytrips to the coast, and spent our free time playing sports or games – I even sang in a choir. Our happiness as a family remained part of our lives too. I never once sensed any worry, nor did I hear the adults mention at all, that the war might affect our lives in any way.

As happened across the whole of Germany, the Nazi regime persecuted Jews in Stralsund. We knew it was happening, of course. One of the girls from my class at school, for instance, suddenly disappeared. But the regime's propaganda was a distraction to keep the remaining population quiet, and soon it all faded into the background. The property belonging to German Jews was damaged or stolen during the so-called *Kristallnacht*, or Night of Broken Glass, and it happened in Stralsund too, particularly on Tribseer Strasse. The public was misled with lies and slogans of hatred, which today we know only too well. It was too easy for us to believe what we were told. Later, when the war was over, I heard about the grisly crimes of the Nazi extermination programme, and had to acknowledge that my uncritical gullibility had played its part in the system too. We were talked into believing that the Jews had been taken to Eastern Europe to work there and establish the German Reich. What a lie! And so we had carried on living our lives without paying any attention to what was going on around us.

In 1940, I left school with my *Mittlere Reife*, my secondary school leaving certificate, and reported for my so-called *Pflichtjahr*, a mandatory year of service. Every girl in Germany had to pass this type of social employment before she could take up an apprenticeship. The responsible authorities allocated me to a position on the Von Hennigs' estate in Techlin, nearly thirty miles southwest of Stralsund. I began my job in 1941, looking after the five Von Hennig children: Renate, Hans-Hermann, Ingrid, Helga, and Fritz. My work was unpaid, but board and lodgings were free. All aspects of life at the manor were strictly disciplined, but even more so where food was concerned. I always ate with the children at the same time as the rest of the family. Eating in the great hall was subject to strict and authoritative rules. Aristocratic guests often visited – visits which seemed to be arranged according to a protocol entirely unknown to me. With the Von Hennigs, I inhabited a world which I'd never known before.

Personally, though, I was treated well, and I think back fondly of my time there. Moreover, it is when I met my friend Annelies, who came from Olbersdorf in Saxony to work on the estate. Ours is a friendship which has lasted until today.

As the year came to a close, I returned to Stralsund to begin my training as a pharmacy assistant. My parents found out from acquaintances of theirs that there was a vacancy in a chemist's in the town. I applied to Mr Ortler, who owned the pharmacy, and was accepted. The practical training was to take place in the pharmacy itself on Ossenreyer Strasse, the main thoroughfare in Stralsund's old town. The shop, Simson Apotheke, still exists now in Mönchstrasse, and was run for many years by Mr Ortler's daughter, Marie-Louise, who was a pharmacist.

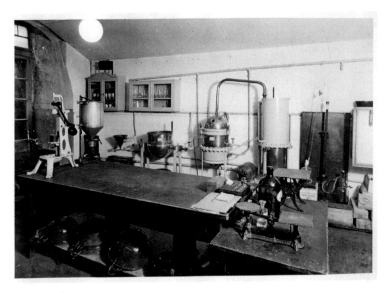

Chemist's workshop in the cellar at Ossenreyer Strasse.
(It was here I was buried during the bombing of 6th October 1944)

I completed my theoretical training at the pharmacy shop in Stralsund. The apprenticeship lasted two years and finished with the exam I had to take at the Apotheken Kammer, the regional centre for pharmaceutical studies, in Stettin – the former capital of what was then Pomerania, but which is now a part of Poland. Originally I had wanted to study pharmacy for the next three years following my apprenticeship, but that wasn't possible any more. The consequences of the ongoing war were making themselves felt. There was a lack of workers, and resources were few. So, for the time being, I carried on working at the chemist's.

The Pharmacy Shop above the cellar.

At the beginning of my apprenticeship, I had been seventeen years old, and the years that followed should have formed a settled sort of framework for me, with the aim of making the transition from sheltered childhood into my own, secure existence – or so I hoped, in any case. This apprenticeship would later, however, influence my life in quite an unexpected way – although of course I never anticipated it at the time.

As a young girl, or a *Fräulein* as we said then, I was occupied by quite different matters. I carried on practising my sports and enjoyed going with my friends to dances, which were sometimes held inside the barracks. I learnt my first dance steps at a course run by the dance school, where my partner was a handsome young man called Fritz. It was the time of teenage infatuation, of first flirtations and kisses – and I certainly had no shortage of affectionate suitors. When I appeared in the barracks, as I came and went each day, the sailors and petty officers would crane their necks. Sometimes, if the sentiments were requited, I would be afflicted with the pounding heartbeat and familiar butterflies' wings, too. Some months previously, my mother had given me a small book to use as a diary, and now I began to write in it at irregular intervals. These little flings filled the book's first pages, and I still have it to this day.

I learnt to play the guitar, too, and it served as an accompaniment to my teenage crushes.

Me (right) with my friend Ursel Vierk (left).

I acquired a two-seater canoe, from a sailor I had befriended, with the proud name Seegraf or 'Lord of the Sea'. In the summer months I used it most, paddling around the Strela Sund, a Baltic lagoon separating the island of Rügen from the German mainland, with my friend Ursel. Our excursions, on which we were often accompanied by other friends, would often finish at the water's edge with a hearty picnic. We'd have a good swim and enjoy some sunbathing, taking in the glorious nature all around us. Another of our favourite summer destinations was the island of Hiddensee, north of Stralsund, unfortunately too far for us to paddle. It's a truly picturesque place that has captivated many famous people, and ordinary folk too. For me, this was a wonderful time.

Carefree days on the Strela Sund.

Meanwhile, though, the war was taking a completely different direction to the one most people had anticipated. It's true that German war propaganda tried to convince the public that the so-called 'Final Victory' was imminent, but the reality was quite different. Prisoners of war were made to work in the barracks where we lived, because German soldiers were falling at the front, which led in turn to the workforces dwindling. Now the regime turned its merciless violence inwards. If you dared to speak out against it in public, or to give anyone cause to doubt your loyalty or devotion to the regime, you risked death in your own country.

I knew from my father that people had been shot on the island of Dänholm, upstream from where we lived; it was apparently not as secret as the executioners had hoped, because fear and terror gradually spread through the population. But nobody wanted to let it show – only in absolute privacy was it safe to express the sympathy that surely comes naturally to any human. My father made sure, though in total secrecy, that living conditions were improved for prisoners of war, giving them access to useful items or food rations. But he was well aware how risky it was. So in time, our old life changed, until, one day, it disappeared altogether – to be replaced with this.

War and the Russian Occupation

At the end of the war and as the Eastern Front drew closer, defeat became a distinct possibility. For the families who lived in our town, life began to change – and it did for us, too. The biggest concern was what form a defeat might take. Would we have to seek refuge in the west? Would we surrender? Would we die? Menacing doubt and fear threatened our daily lives. More and more soldiers returned home from the front, and thousands of refugees arrived in Stralsund from East Prussia and Transpomerania, both of which are now part of Poland. Young women were trained and recruited to help the Red Cross to deal with the emergency, and I was among them.

It was 1944, just a year before the war ended. I was about twenty years old, still working at the Simson *Apotheke* (chemist), when the terror of war suddenly reached us.

On 6th October, I went to work at the pharmacy, as I did every day. In recent weeks, Stralsund had been threatened by bombers – the Americans by day and the British at night – their approach announced by howling sirens. We ran to the closest air raid shelter. On this particular day, it was around midday when the sirens began to cry. Everyone who worked in the pharmacy went immediately down to the laboratory in the cellar, which served as our air raid shelter. But that day, we didn't just hear the drones of the bombers flying overhead – we felt very clearly the bombs exploding around us. The whole building shook, the noise of the tremors combining with that of the squadron overhead. Now it was certain that Stralsund was under attack from the air. What was happening outside now? What would happen to us? To our misfortune, the pharmacy building was hit and completely destroyed – and we were trapped in the cellar. We listened out for every sound to judge as best we could exactly what was going on above us. It was quickly and terrifyingly clear to us that every way out of the cellar was blocked by fallen masonry. The air raid had only lasted a few minutes, but now began a long wait, full of trepidation, to be freed of the rubble. All of us, including my friend Ursel who was there, tried to get the rescuers' attention by banging and shouting. After many hours of veering from hope to despair and back again, it worked - the soldiers who were sent out to rescue people finally reached the cellar where we were trapped, just after six o'clock in the evening. Thankfully none of us had life-threatening injuries.

Ossenreyerstr. 6th Oct 1944.
By Permission Stralsund Town Archive.

We were all alive and relieved to get out the cellar, but outside the town was unrecognisable. The row of houses next to our building had been completely destroyed. The streets were full of corpses and the wounded. Everywhere there was rubble, smoke, and the acrid smell of burning. People wandered through the ruins, crying – looking for their loved ones, for their homes, or their belongings.

The day leaned eventually into the darkness of the night. I couldn't tell you how I managed to get home. Dazed and disconnected from reality, I reached our flat in the barracks after seven o'clock that evening. Miraculously, it was undamaged. In the days that followed, the extent of the devastation became more and more apparent. The effects of the bombing were clear to see in the Franken suburbs and the area around the harbour in the old town. By some miracle, Stralsund's two great churches, St. Marien and St. Nikolai, were left standing. Only the church of St. Jacobi was badly damaged, like many of the houses in neighbouring Heilgeiststrasse. And of my canoe, which I had always kept in the little boatyard near the Heilgeist monastery, only ruins were left.

Ossenreyerstr. 6th Oct 1944.
By Permission Stralsund Town Archive.

Only slowly were we able to recover from this shock, which had turned our lives upside-down in just a few minutes. Nevertheless, we guessed that this was to be just the very beginning of the end.

The dead, killed in the bombing raid, were brought to the barracks' parade ground, right next to our home, to be identified by their relatives. The image of hundreds of bodies lying there is seared into my mind to this day. One of the victims was Dr Kummer, who had been killed as she worked in her surgery on Semlowerstrasse, where we used to live, on the corner of Mauerstrasse. The house next door, where we had lived during 1936 and '37, was completely destroyed. It was only by lucky coincidence that we no longer lived there.

*Ruins at Heilgeiststrasse 75. The shop of my friend Anneliese Friedrichs
on the right edge.
By Permission Stralsund Town Archive.*

An immediate consequence of the bombing of Stralsund was that the civilian population was evacuated to surrounding communities, if they had not already moved, and if it was not absolutely necessary

for them to stay in the town. My mother and siblings were taken
in by a Frau Splitter, who lived in Niepars. Only my father and I
stayed behind in the flat in Stralsund, because we still had to go
to work. After being unemployed for a short while – because the
pharmacy where I had worked no longer existed – I was set to work
as a prospective pharmacist and trained Red Cross assistant, dealing
with the typhus patients at the specially designated quarantine
barracks on Weidendamm, in the centre of Stralsund.

In my Red Cross uniform.

In January 1945, Herr Stubenhofer, who had managed the Simson
pharmacy, reopened the shop on Mönchstrasse, and I took up my
job there again. By the end of February, however, the events of the
war and the ever-closer Eastern Front had disrupted the rhythm of
everyday life. Everybody had to face the question: how would they
and their loved ones pull through it? What would the end of the
war mean for them? Those who were able fled to the west. Together
with the other Red Cross girls, I treated wounded soldiers returning
from the front in the last months of the war. We had to do the work
– it was compulsory, and how could it have been any different in
the circumstances? Nobody was interested in whether we enjoyed
the work or not. Thoughts of what was yet to come filled us with
uncertainty and fear.

Businesses were closing all over Stralsund for fear of the
Russian advance. Before the chemist's shop closed, our boss made

us an offer: he would give us as much potassium cyanide powder as we would need for ourselves, and each member of our family, 'just in case'. The 'Final Victory or Death' propaganda was having a definite impact on the population. If it came to such, every person was supposed to see suicide as a preferable option to defeat. I took up my boss' offer, and so did my colleagues. We had no idea what was to come. Both reports from the east and the propaganda of Hitler's regime spoke only of death, separation, looting, and rape. If we lived, we wouldn't be able to escape any of these threats. I gave the poison from the chemist to my mother, and she locked it in a cabinet in our makeshift home in Niepars. After that, nothing more was said about it.

Then came the very last days of the war. Because the pharmacy had closed, I stayed with my family in Niepars. Only my father was ordered to stay behind at the barracks in Stralsund.

White cloths or sheets were hung outside every house as a sign of surrender. On 1st May 1945, the Russians arrived. That day, my father walked to Niepars from Stralsund, nine miles away, covered in blood and in ripped, filthy clothes. The Stralsund barracks had been taken over by Polish units, and he had dragged himself back to Niepars after they had taken him prisoner and beaten him. He was forced to gather together women of all ages who would then be raped by the soldiers. When he arrived at home, he was in deep distress. Now the whole family was here together, including my grandmother.

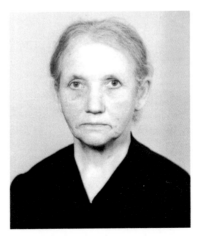

My grandmother Martha Schmidt, née Kosbahn.

23

When my father arrived in Niepars, it was already late afternoon, and night gradually began to fall. Horrific, dramatic scenes were being played out across the whole of the village. The Red Army's soldiers broke into the houses, looting them, and raping the women. The people fled if they could and, as I later found out, some threw themselves into the Pütter See, a nearby lake. We could hear people screaming and shots being fired, and a crippling fear gripped us. There was no hope any more. Nobody wanted the morning to come.

I don't think that my mother had planned what happened next. In that desperate situation, she must have seen it as the only way out. She took the cyanide powder from the cupboard, but my father was not completely sure — he still disagreed. The situation came to a head. Darkness had fallen totally now, and the shouts and cries for help were growing louder as the Russian soldiers worked their way down each street. It must have been somewhere around eight o'clock in the evening. My mother mixed the poison with water and divided into glasses for us to drink. One glass fell to the floor and smashed. She told me that she wanted to share hers with me. But it was as though I was paralysed — I couldn't think clearly any more. She gave seven-year-old Klausi his glass first. I heard him cry, so pitifully, "Mutti, I don't want to die." But the decision had been made. Mother gave out the glasses to the others, each filled with the deadly poison: to Helga, Peter, our grandmother, and our father. A few minutes later, the rattling of their death throes could be heard. It was horrific.

I still had to find a definite solution for myself — I didn't want to be left on my own. I remembered then that my mother kept Luminal sleeping pills in the house. Consumed with terror, I searched for them and eventually found them. In the meantime, my mother had drunk her poison and lay on the bed. As the only one left alive, I closed their open eyes and bade farewell to this world with a hastily written scribble in a notebook. Then I took twenty Luminal tablets as I heard the Russians shouting and hammering on the door. I was still on my feet as the first of them broke in and hit me in the face with the butt of a rifle. Then I fell unconscious.

On the note, I had written:

May you live a life free of pain, you dear people, you who are condemned to live on. Send our love one last time to those who ask after us. Let us be together even in death. We are free!

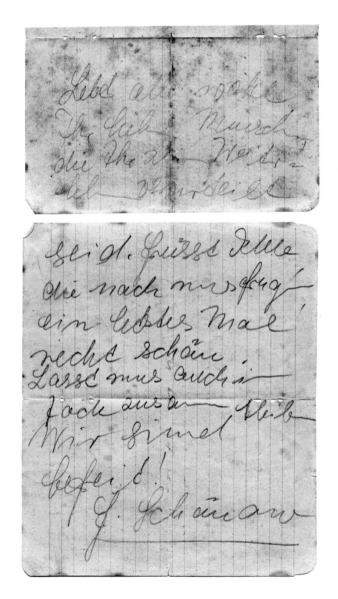

I thought these would be my last words.

Five days later, I awoke in a bed in a neighbour's house. My mind and my senses immediately began to work again, and the images of my family dying came back to me. But I took a moment to assess my condition. My front teeth had been knocked out, my nose was broken, and my hair was matted with blood – everything hurt. The leather jacket, my shoes, and the jodhpurs I had been wearing were all missing. But I hadn't been raped. As I noticed in the mirror some time later, my whole face was black – the Luminal must have caused that. The mirror had been covered up at first, because I had been so maimed and disfigured. I wasn't supposed to look at my reflection. A Russian soldier was present at all times, and so I was being watched. That had to be arranged for my own safety, though, because any attempt to escape would have been unthinkable on my part.

I was the only member of my family left – I considered my survival to be part of my fate; an unwanted part. I was utterly bereft. Somebody had chosen to save me, but why? Only the rest of my life could answer that question. The first moments of realisation had been terrible, because I had previously chosen to end my life. I didn't have the strength to resist fate. In the days that followed, I learnt from the Russians billeted here, who were officers and aides-de-camp of the occupation army, that the Russian strike force had left Niepars on the same day, and that the army doctor had been called when they discovered that I was still alive. He was close at hand, because the aides-de-camp who rushed ahead had chosen the house as a temporary billet for the officers. I was told that the doctor had brought me back to life, removing the tablets from my stomach by turning me upside down and shaking me until everything that had been in my stomach came out. I think it more likely my stomach was pumped, or I was induced to vomit. Luckily I was able to communicate with the doctor, who came from Tbilisi in Georgia, because he was fluent in German. I was told that my family were in Stralsund, obviously by way of reassuring me. But I didn't believe it, because I knew that it wasn't so. To get them out of the house, they had been buried by the Russians outside in the garden. They lay in the holes that we had dug ourselves, the night before, to hide our valuables. Those possessions, of course, had disappeared.

The doctor was finally able to move me to the schoolhouse that had once belonged to a Herr Voss, on what used to be Langensaal (today called Schulstrasse). It was empty now. Here he oversaw my care by a nurse, Ilse Ohlrich, who I knew well, and gradually, some of my personal belongings were returned to me: my family's photo albums, for example, which were found on the street. That's how I got my diary back too, and a dress of mine. I wore it straightaway, as I had nothing else to wear.

Gradually I came back to life – albeit under the totally different auspices of the Russians. I had no will to live anymore; I merely existed. I did not feel grateful that I had been rescued. After around two weeks, my recovery had progressed such that I asked the doctor to take me to my relatives in Stralsund, Frieda and Hermann Kühn. He organised my transport there. Their flat on Langenstrasse was small, and partly damaged by bombs. I was allowed to stay with my aunt and uncle there in Stralsund. When I first stood before them, they didn't recognise me, for I still looked so disfigured.

"Oh my God!" my aunt cried out. She gathered me to her and hugged me tight. At some point in the following days, I must have written in my diary about the events of 1st May and what happened afterwards. If I read those pages today, my voice breaks and chokes.

Aunt Frieda and Uncle Hermann from Stralsund.

At the beginning of June 1945, the unit with the Georgian doctor withdrew from Niepars. Before he left, he came to see us in Stralsund, provided us with cash and some food, and issued my aunt and uncle with a certificate about my treatment. It was a very humane gesture at such a time. But that was not the last time I met that man, Temo Melikidse, as would later be revealed. I can still hear his words in my ear:

"We'll see each other again. I'll come back!"

The certificate attested that I had been treated by a doctor from the Red Army, and had been declared sick and therefore unable to work. The Russian part was validated by the occupying Red Army soldiers, and its German counterpart by the German authorities. But I never had to show this proof that I was ill.

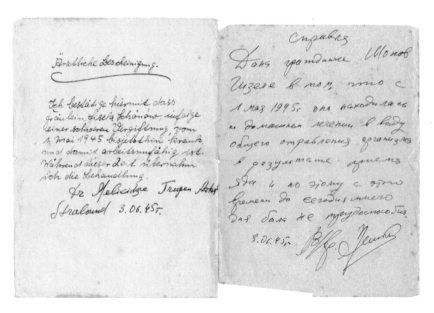

My note from the doctor, in German (left) and in Russian (right).

I can hereby confirm that Miss Gisela Schönow, as a consequence of serious poisoning, has been ill from 1st May 1945 until now, and as such is unable to work. During this time, she was treated by me.
Dr. Melikidse, Stralsund 3/6/45

I was still suffering from shock, though. I think that I eventually found the strength to carry on because I was young and strong, and optimistic, in a manner of speaking.

On 7th June 1945, it was my father's birthday. I went back to Niepars with my aunt and uncle, taking a handcart with us, to bury our dead family members in the cemetery there. We unearthed them from the garden behind our house, and took them on the handcart to the cemetery, where they were buried close to the church with the permission of the Reverend Prolius. My grandmother was buried alongside her husband, who had died some years earlier. We dismantled a wardrobe to use as makeshift coffins. I can't remember anymore quite how I managed to do it – I must have been completely desensitised to it. Later, I arranged to have a headstone erected on the grave, and if you visited the cemetery today, it would never occur to you that such a tragedy had taken place there.

My family's headstone in the cemetery at Niepars.

Incidentally, I never ever went back to my parents' flat in the barracks, even though the building remained standing and eventually more of the family's personal effects were found there. I didn't want to taint the memory of my real, living, whole images of my father, my mother, and my brothers and sisters by setting foot in the empty, looted rooms.

On the same day that we were in Niepars re-burying my family, the Georgian doctor returned to Langenstrasse in Stralsund – I hadn't believed that he would keep his promise. He left behind more food and money for us, giving everything to Frau Busch, the landlady, who handed it over to us when we returned.

In the following months, particularly in the winter of 1945 and '46, every person had to fight just to survive. Stralsund had been utterly destroyed. Many people were still looking for missing relatives. The refugees who arrived in Stralsund from the east, or those who were just passing through, were given emergency shelter and medical care. I remember going with my aunt through the thick, creaking snow to the harbour at around one o'clock in the morning to gather up briquettes which were lying about – small blocks made of coal dust or peat, which we burned for fuel. This was dangerous work, because the Russians had organised guards and watchmen. In the town, where people were desperate, the black market boomed. We would swap, for instance, bed sheets for bread, or collect potato peelings from the rubbish, thrown out by the Russians, to cook soup. Spread for bread, instead of butter, was made with flour, water, and a little thyme. Because of our poor diet, I got scabies. Many people were infested with lice, which you could see because they would wear a louse cap on their heads.

Typhus, too, spread like the plague through the town. Patients were treated in the barracks at Weidendamm, which had been part of the former hospital. It was here, from August 1945, that I was employed to care for the sick. There were fewer and fewer people left to care for them, because so many people were dying. It didn't take long before I had caught typhus too. On 26th September, I became a patient at the barracks myself. Thankfully, I was able to leave on 27th October, having recovered, and returned to my aunt and uncle.

Although we were occupied and many German soldiers were injured or imprisoned, life had to go on. The Russian occupation force had set up their quarters in the town. The commandant's office was down on the August-Bebel riverbank, just by the Frankenteich, a pond in the centre of Stralsund, bordered on one side by the

Weidendamm. Officers were housed in Grosse Parower Strasse, near the naval hospital. The town's authorities were beginning to start up their administration again – albeit in completely different circumstances.

Ruins

My life up until that point, and the home that had made me feel safe, had been totally destroyed. I had overcome neither my own trauma of what had happened at Niepars, nor my burgeoning guilt for bringing the poison home from the chemist's. Would my family still have been alive if it hadn't been for that poison, or would they have met an even worse end? The question still tortured me.

Some nights I just cried; my tears could have filled entire lakes. How could I go on? How could I go back to living a normal – or even a bearable – life? To me, it seemed completely impossible. The only way, I thought, would be to throw myself into work, work, and more work. That might heal my wounded, empty soul, and stop those harrowing images from filling my head. But it only partly succeeded.

In comparison to the town's ruins, my own inner destruction was invisible. I felt as though I had been actually hollowed out, that I would be marked forever by my losses. Nobody could free me of that pain. I did what I had to do to keep myself alive, but inside, I had lost my family, my house, my entire homeland – really, I had lost myself. I became desperate. Only gradually could I come to terms with what had happened. My thoughts drifted here and there, searching aimlessly for a place to rest.

Fleeing my own country

On 19th April 1946, I began an assistantship at the surgery of a Dr Stroehlein on the Jungfernstieg in Stralsund, which had been found for me through the unemployment office. Dr Stroehlein had been an army doctor, who practised as an internist. It was not to be a long-term post for me, though, because he died of cancer in January the following year. The surgeon who had treated him, Dr Wendt, took me on as his receptionist at the beginning of February 1947. I was already familiar with working in a surgery, but I also had to assist him when he took X-rays in the radiography rooms on the Jungfernstieg.

As well as providing me with an income, working at Dr Wendt's surgery meant that my life was more varied now, and I slowly found that there was more of a point to everyday tasks. The surgery was at An den Bleichen 6, and belonged to the doctor's parents-in-law, the Mahnke family. Dr Wendt was well-known in his field; he had worked previously at the Charité Hospital in Berlin with the noted Professor Sauerbruch, who had been a pioneer of heart and lung operations throughout the early decades of the twentieth century. The occupying Russian forces trusted him. Because he lived in the same building as the surgery, I also knew his wife and their three children. I worked up to twelve hours a day and learnt about a great many new things, like laboratory work and administering drugs. Dr Wendt was very ambitious in his work, and had a tendency to be demanding. At first I couldn't quite meet his high standards. I made mistakes, but once Dr Wendt had corrected me several times, I improved quite quickly.

The longer I worked for Dr Wendt, the more responsibility I was given. Eventually, I was assisting him with minor operations on Russian soldiers or on local residents of Stralsund. Sometimes this involved helping to anaesthetise patients using the old method of applying drops of ether to a face mask – today I wonder how I managed all of this without a catastrophic outcome for the patients.

But my work was not my entire life. During the evenings, I had to take care of Aunt Frieda and Uncle Hermann, neither of whom was particularly young. At some point around this time, they were moved into the same convent in which my grandmother had spent her last years. Now I lived all alone in the little flat on Langenstrasse.

The work at the doctor's surgery increased to such an extent that Dr Wendt began looking to employ another person to help us. I told my canoeing friend Ursel Vierk about the vacancy – she was working in the meantime at a chemist's in Garz, on the island of Rügen. She was interested in the job and so Dr Wendt decided to hire her. We shared out the work between us and went home together at the end of the day. This change, working with Ursel, meant that now I had some sort of life outside work. We found a distraction, though, taking trips to Rügen and Hiddensee again, or going to dances at the Hotel zum Bahnhof, next to the railway station. We were accompanied by Ursel's mother, as was proper in those days for young women. There were even a few interested men there, who flirted with me. That was definitely a pleasant feeling, but I didn't want to be tied down – and nor could I spare any of my time.

We received fabric from Ursel's relatives which they sent to us from West Berlin, so that we could make dresses with it. Back then, we depended on a certain 'do-it-yourself' attitude, because there were no shops with ready-made goods to sell. Other things required a little improvisation and skill too. Thankfully, my family had taught me to put in a bit of elbow grease.

One day, a friend of mine, Annelies, arrived at my door from her home in Saxony. I had met her at the Von Hennigs' manor house in Techlin in 1941, but in the confusion of the end of the war and the time that followed, we had lost touch. But she had asked how to get to Stralsund and, eventually, found her way to me. So we were connected once more. I even attended her wedding in her hometown of Olbersdorf, near Zittau, in January 1951. After that, we never lost touch again.

Slowly, our eyes were opened to the social conditions of our occupation, and the political powers in the former eastern zone; we realised that we were not supposed to live individual lives, according to our own free will. Inevitably, that led to repression, and people began to head off in the direction of the west. Because it was mainly the young, motivated people who left, that led in turn to further shortages. Predominantly young people, among whom I counted myself of course, looked to escape from the collapsed social order, to find their own paths out of the post-war crisis. We had no guidance; everyone tried to do what they could, for instance with information they'd accidentally overheard, or just at their own discretion. Once I had managed to make some sense of the worst days of my young life, I too wanted to make a change for myself. But how should I start? What would be the right way to go about it? I thought about the young Georgian doctor, T. Melikidse, for whom I had to thank for my survival and who was obviously very fond of me. He had promised me more than once that we would see each other again. If the circumstances had allowed in 1945, perhaps I might even have gone with him. In hindsight, perhaps that would have been a mistake, but at the time it seemed to me to be one way out. And so, now some years after the war had ended, I made the decision to write to him. I wanted to find out for myself whether this man really did want to have a deeper connection with me, or whether I should give up on that completely. He had written down his civilian address in Tiflis – now known as Tbilisi – for me, so I wrote him a letter in the hope that he might be able to make sense of things for me. But I had no reply. That was in 1949. Either he had never received the letter, I supposed, or I had not received his answer. I tried once more, and then I tried again by telegram. But still it was the same – no answer. From then on, I never expected him to get in touch with me, nor that I would ever see him again, and my thoughts and feelings about him gradually settled down.

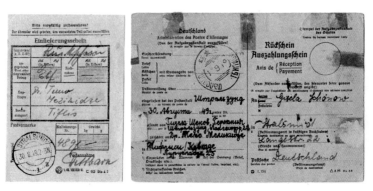

My receipt of postage and return receipt.

35

The situation in West Germany at that time was not so dissimilar to that in the East, but very soon the two parts of the country began to take different directions to one another. In any case, I thought or at least hoped that the way to freedom would be straightforward from the West. Twice I made the journey with Ursel and her mother to what was then the British sector of Germany – later *Niedersachsen* or Lower Saxony – where Ursel's married sister lived. We did it illegally and, to cross the river Elbe, we had to pay the border smugglers. It was the same on the way back, but there were checks by the Russians too, who were very rough. Nevertheless, we got back to Stralsund unharmed.

On these trips, I began to think about the possible ways in which I might be able to leave the East. With my training as a pharmacy assistant, and my experience of working at a doctor's surgery, I contemplated working for a charity organisation in the so called 'Third World'. However Germans could not apply for that sort of work yet.

By now the Eastern, Russian controlled, zone of Germany had become the German Democratic Republic, or the GDR, formed officially in 1949. It was more commonly known in the west as East Germany. It was clear that anyone leaving to travel abroad was viewed as 'running away', with no possibility of return in the foreseeable future.

My biggest problem remained: how to make my escape? I had to be careful who I confided in and how I organised this during the years of 1950-1951. I needed help but could only tell friends and relatives if I believed them to be totally discrete and reliable.

I spoke to Dr Wendt about my thoughts, hopes and plans. He helped me contact the Catholic charity Caritas based in the Charlottenburg area of what had become West Berlin. I was not allowed to travel to West Berlin; however Dr Wendt had a permit to go there. He had this in order for him to make monthly trips to Berlin, with his wife, to collect drugs and medical supplies that he needed to treat the Russian officers. On these trips he acquired the application forms from Caritas for me, returning them when I had completed them. By doing so he was also taking a big risk, for which I am eternally grateful. Because of my increasing experience at his surgery, and I like to think my good work, he did not want me to go. He did however understand my reasons for wanting to leave, which is why he begrudgingly helped me.

At the time the only jobs offered were in childcare. One of these positions was as an au pair to a farming family in Cornwall with three children, and something similar in Scotland. It must have been September 1950, and I felt I needed to seize the opportunity. I applied for the job in Cornwall. Soon thereafter my application was accepted. A Mr Vernon from Wadebridge would pay my travel costs and a date was agreed. I was to go to Britain and work for him for one year.

Without me asking Caritas also allocated me a job for the following year in Windhoek, in what was then German Southwest Africa, today of course Namibia. They did this as they knew another German girl they had placed there previously would be leaving. Although I knew virtually nothing about the country the most important thing was that it would give me another year of work after Wadebridge. The first concrete steps of my escape were now in place!

Before I embarked upon my great journey, I visited my friend Annelies in Olbersdorf. She and her new husband Martin had invited me to their wedding, on 15th January 1951. It was a wonderful trip – I saw many lovely, familiar faces. But I knew already that I wanted to take a very different direction with my life.

When the day of my definite departure arrived, 17th February 1951, I was full of hope and yet melancholy at the same time. I had been disadvantaged by my circumstances in East Germany, and I most certainly wanted to change that. In that sense, I gathered within me as much hope as I could muster. But the melancholy was still there too. I was leaving the place where I had played out my entire life up until that point – and, more to the point, I was leaving secretly, and for such a long time. I didn't know what lay ahead of me. I was leaving behind friends and relatives – everybody who was dearest to me, who also cared for me. One of my relatives, Albert Küster from Peterblome Strasse, who worked on the railway, accompanied me to the station as he was working that night. He had recommended that I catch the late train to Berlin, because he knew that there wouldn't be the usual checks imposed by the Russians on night-time journeys to the capital – the city of the four occupying forces, Britain, the US, France, and Russia – as there were during the daytime. Everything ran smoothly. But if I had been caught, I'd have been imprisoned in Neubrandenburg, which lay between Stralsund and Berlin. It was a great risk to take. I must have blocked it out. The occupying Russians had a camp there, where they detained Nazis and alleged Nazis, the people they saw as enemies. You couldn't count on either mercy or justice.

But I also want to say a bit about what happened later that evening as I travelled to Berlin. I knew from working at the surgery a relatively young widower, called Paul Schmidt. I always had a lot of contact with him, because he came regularly to Dr Wendt's surgery with an injury from an accident. We found each other likeable, and I also knew that he had a two-year-old daughter and lived in Kleine Diebsteig, not far from the Frankendamm in Stralsund. Once he had even fixed my bicycle for me, but beyond that we didn't see each other. Frau Busch, the owner of Langenstrasse 22, the house where I lived until I left East Germany, told me later that only around an hour after I had left, a man came to ask after me. He had introduced himself as Paul Schmidt and, I'm reliably informed, wanted to propose to me. In hindsight, I can't say how I would have answered if he had asked me earlier. So I was saved the decision, and fate took me down a very different path.

Now, back to my journey. I arrived at a station in Berlin in the early hours of 18th February 1951. It was icy cold and still dark. My excitement was growing. I – and my luggage – had to get onto an S-Bahn, part of Berlin's urban railway, to Charlottenburg. Everything went smoothly and I arrived at the Caritas charity. There I was given my plane ticket to Hamburg, Mr Vernon's address in Wadebridge, and the rest of my connections and travel dates for the journey. In addition, I was given a new identification card with a limited period of validity, which had already been prepared. Ursel Vierk's aunt, who lived in Charlottenburg, had sorted it all out. I only had to 'stamp' my right index finger on the document, and sign it. The identification card was essential, so that I could leave Germany legally.

My temporary identification card from West Berlin.

My flight from Berlin-Gatow, a former British RAF airfield in the southwest of the city, to Hamburg left on the same day. I boarded the plane as its twenty-eighth passenger, and found that there was real coffee on board, as well as such luxuries as cakes, ham, and chocolate. After one-and-a-quarter hours, we reached Hamburg airport. My journey continued from there by bus to Ballindamm, in the city centre, where I was met by an employee from the Catholic network St. Raphael's. I would not be travelling any further until the following day, a Monday, and so I stayed overnight at a Catholic welfare organisation, on Papenhuder Strasse. I had to spend the night in a hall with seventeen other young women, who I thought were street girls, and whose priority was not nice things like flowery cardigans anymore. I was worried about the few possessions that I had brought with me, and so I didn't get much sleep. But in the end, I and my luggage survived unscathed. On Monday morning at half past ten, I boarded another train, alone. Shortly beforehand, I had handed in my heavy fifty-pound suitcase at customs, to be taken on to London. The train came from Scandinavia, and its destination was the port town of Hoek van Holland, in the Netherlands. My fellow passengers came from all over Europe, which certainly impressed me, because until then I'd never known anything like it.

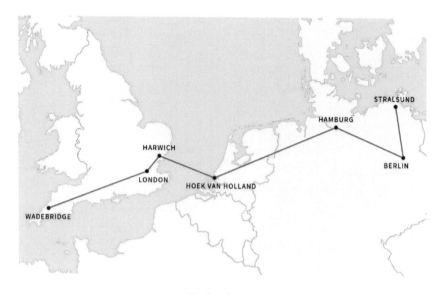

Gisela's Journey.
© *OpenStreetMap contributors.*

The following evening, I embarked on the next stage of my journey, the crossing to Harwich in England. It was still very cold, and unfortunately stormy too. To top it all off, I was seasick, and had to stay on deck, clutching the railing. Some of the more sympathetic members of the crew looked after me and took me below deck. I was so ill that I would have thrown myself in the sea if I could. A few of my fellow travellers gave me something to eat, so that I was able to get through the rest of the journey. By morning, at around six or seven o'clock, we had arrived in England. Now I had to take the train to London. Again, there were more sympathetic passengers in the carriage. They commented that I didn't have any food with me, and offered me bits and pieces, including treasures like oranges. They listened while I told them why and where I was going, and where I came from. A very kind gentleman gave me some coins, including a half-crown, as they were then – around £3.50 in today's money. I was very grateful and thought that I was now rich; sadly that wasn't the case. The train arrived at Liverpool

Street. Now I was in London, this vast and vibrant city, and I was overwhelmed. The Catholic charity had told me that the trains to Cornwall go from Waterloo.

Out on the street, I hailed a taxi – some of the people on the train had suggested that I do so, because I wasn't familiar with the underground, and wouldn't be able to get my bearings. Eventually, one stopped.

"Waterloo Station, please!" I said in my German accent. Whatever the driver uttered in reply I had no idea, but I got into the taxi. On arrival I held out my hand to present my coins to him, to show that I could pay my fare. He stared, astonished.

"Is that all you have?"

I replied that it was.

"Never mind!" he said, laughing, and drove off. He probably didn't have a passenger like me every day. It was my second experience of friendliness in England, after my companions on the train.

At the station, though, I was met with bad news – my suitcase, which I had handed in at customs in Hamburg, hadn't arrived. I was quite shocked. Though the case didn't contain any valuables, it was full of my work things, aprons and special personal items which I'd certainly need in Wadebridge. That was an unexpected setback for me. I began to sob. A railway official heard me, and comforted me. He explained that that the suitcase wasn't lost, but it would arrive later and be sent on. I found that hard to believe, because at that time I hadn't any experience of travelling abroad. But there was nothing more I could do. To this day I remember sitting and crying under the large clock in the centre of Waterloo station, which is still there today.

The official was so very kind to me, taking me to my train, because he quickly realised that I didn't know what I was doing. And so I encountered more friendliness from the English. He asked whether I had brought anything with me to eat – I must have looked quite wretched. When I said I hadn't, he bought me some food at a bistro. Then he put me on the train.

"Now you'll go on to Wadebridge!" he said. And so I did; the journey took some hours.

When I finally arrived, I was met at the station by Mr Vernon, the farmer who I would be working for. I got off the train and heard an unfamiliar voice, shouting:

"Miss Schönow, where is Miss Schönow?"

"Here!" I replied. The station in Wadebridge was small and straightforward to navigate, and so we quickly found each other. This was the man, then, who had, without knowing me, 'ordered' me from Germany, so to speak.

And so I had arrived at my destination – I was relieved to finally be here. Mr Vernon had flown with the RAF, and become a farmer by marriage. He took me in his Jeep to Wadebridge police station, where I had to register. My finger print was taken, and my passport was as well. Then, at about midnight, we reached the farm, Dunveth, at the top of Whiterock Road, where the town blends into the surrounding farmland. The farmer's family took me into their farmhouse. Though it was late, Mr Vernon still wanted to go out to a party, and hurriedly showed me the children's room.

"This is Peter, this is Patricia, and this is Michael – and this is your room! See you tomorrow!"

Now I was here; this would be home for at least a year. Only, my suitcase wasn't there. That's always stuck with me, because I urgently needed a few things from it, to settle into my room and make it feel homely. I was dreadfully homesick and besides, it was embarrassing to be there without my belongings. Thankfully, these days such situations would be much easier to avoid.

The Vernons treated me fairly, even though the work I had to do was very hard. On the day of my arrival, I was woken at six o'clock – that was the beginning of my new life. And, after all that, my suitcase arrived at the farm two days later. Thoughts of Stralsund, my home, stayed with me, as did my thoughts of the people closest to me – particularly Aunt Frieda and Uncle Hermann – even though my links to them had been interrupted, for the moment at least. In spite of this, I was sure that I had taken the right step. That has remained the right decision to this day.

A New Home

Now Wadebridge, a small Cornish town on the River Camel, was my new home. The river snakes its way down in bights from the nearby Bodmin Moor, through the surrounding hills. It flows through Wadebridge from the south to the north, and is mostly shallow; near Padstow, on the northern coast, it reaches the Atlantic. The river's current, its ebb and flow, helps to shape the landscape until it reaches its destination at the coast, some seven miles from the town. The town itself, now home to around seven thousand people, is surrounded by farmland – a former market town, from days when agriculture was one of the most important economic sectors in the county of Cornwall. Much earlier, it was mining, and later tourism would become an important influence on the county's towns and countryside.

Bill Vernon's farm was located on the western edge of the town, on a hill from which you had a clear view over the valley and the hillsides opposite. If the visibility was good, you could see to the east both of the moor's highest peaks, Brown Willy and Rough Tor. The town itself was, and still is, characterised by the old stone bridge, straddling the Camel River, which gave it its name.

The Old Stone Bridge.
Courtesy of ©Adrian Langdon.

Wadebridge developed on either side of the river, with the town centre on the western side, with its main streets being Molesworth Street and The Platt.

The history of the bridge in Wadebridge.

On the surface, the countryside is covered in greenery, but the ground beneath contains much slate and granite. This landscape was certainly very different to the one I knew in Pomerania – and so was the climate. I didn't realise that properly until later, because in the beginning I had to concern myself with quite different things. In the first moments after my arrival in Wadebridge, I never suspected that I would spend the rest of my life there.

First and foremost, I had to settle in with the Vernons, find my bearings on the farm, and familiarise myself with the tasks that were assigned to me. My knowledge of English was sufficient to make myself understood – it was a good job I'd paid attention at school. My main job was to look after the children, just as I had in Techlin before the war. The Vernons' children – there were three at the time, Patricia, Peter, and Michael – were aged three years, two years, and six months old respectively - and it seemed to me that they were not too accustomed to discipline, or not as I had known it in Germany.

But caring for the children was not the only duty I was given by the family. Mr Vernon also roped me in to help with the milking, which I first had to learn how to do, and for work in the fields. This was all new to me, but I did my best, and even learnt to drive the tractor and drill machine over the field.

"I need Gisela now in the field!" Mr Vernon would always say to his wife, when he wanted to get me away from the children.

Then the children would stay with their mother. The work lasted into the evening – truth be told, until about ten o'clock at night – after which I would fall into bed, deadbeat. There was a rumour on the farm that ghosts were said to haunt my room. That never spooked me, though, and I always fell asleep straightaway.

I can't describe properly how I felt in this period, just after arriving in England – as though I was being controlled from the outside, perhaps. At the same time, a little of the hope that had led me to Cornwall still remained. I dedicated myself completely to my work, just as I had in Stralsund, trying to fill the emptiness which opened up again, so as not to let it swallow me. I wasn't plagued by fear or worry, because I wanted to find myself again, in a manner of speaking. Whether I would succeed remained to be seen.

The entrance to the Vernons' farm in 2015.

The Vernons began to appreciate me for the work I did. But in spite of that, I still felt that I came from 'enemy territory'. On several occasions, I heard people call me obviously unpleasant names. But others were friendly towards me. They compensated for the bad behaviour, and made me feel – gradually – like I belonged. At the start, as I remember very well, I wandered the winding, narrow streets with a little book that I had brought with me from Stralsund, reading German poetry aloud to myself, like my favourite pieces by Goethe and Schiller.

Mrs Vernon, whose first name was Joan, had been keen on horses when she was young, and she had kept her riding gear. I was familiar with the sport from the years before the war, and so of course I was very interested in picking it up again here. One day she let me have her jodhpurs, and I was also able to borrow a hack from the Prideaux-Brune estate near Padstow, so I was able to start riding again, slowly but surely.

There is one small incident, though, which I haven't forgotten. In post-war Germany, particularly in East Germany in the early years, food was very scarce, and so I was used to eating any food when it came along, scraping my plate. It was virtually impossible to get hold of treats. The Vernons often had chocolate pudding, which I liked very much. Sometimes the children would leave their food half-finished, or barely even touch it. Whatever was left would go in the bin, but I couldn't understand that, and asked to eat the rest; the Vernons were obviously surprised.

Gradually, because of all the errands I was tasked with by the Vernons, I got to know the other people in the little town, mostly through the connections Mr Vernon had to other business people in the area, who were useful to his work on the farm. By the time a few weeks had passed, I had made the effort to get to know the town and the people who lived there.

Quite unexpectedly, one of these contacts changed my life completely, at a startling speed. Mr Hamilton Hawkey owned the petrol station, and Mr Vernon went to him for the fuel for his cars, tractors, and machinery. And so it was to him that I had to go most often. The petrol station, called Toll-Gate, bordered Mr Vernon's farm, in a north-westerly direction from Wadebridge, near a place known locally as Toll House Corner. Mr Hawkey's petrol station included a workshop, and a small shop for snacks, sweets, chocolate, ice cream, and all the other little things people want on long journeys. There I spent the money I had earned – which was seventeen shillings and sixpence a week, as well as my ration coupons – with the sole aim of sending the goodies back to Stralsund, to Aunt Frieda and Uncle Hermann, because I knew they couldn't buy such things in Germany. Mr Hawkey realised what I was doing, often giving me a little extra, and helping me to pack up the little parcels. He seemed touched that I thought so much of my relatives.

Wadebridge, my new home.
Courtesy of ©Adrian Langdon.

It didn't escape me either that Hamilton felt increasingly comfortable in my presence. After a certain amount of time, he began to court me. The attention did me good, but inside I didn't think it would last. My work and so my time in Wadebridge were both limited to one year; after that, I would have to move immediately on to Windhoek, my placement in Africa. But, once again, my life worked out differently; thankfully this time it was for very happy reasons. Hamilton sought my company more and more – we spent time babysitting together, for example, while the Vernons went to a party. When the summer came, he invited me on trips to the Cornish coast, in his car. These were happy days for me, after a long time. We got to know each other better and I learnt that Hamilton, who was eighteen years older than me, had separated from his first wife some time ago, and was divorced. He had no children of his own.

Only my own existing plans stood in the way of our relationship. I needed a while to assess my situation.

One day, Hamilton and I went to the coast alone, to Bedruthan Steps, a place we both knew and loved. It is a steep, towering cliff on the north coast, with a wide sandy beach exposed at low tide. There, Hamilton wrote in huge letters in the sand.

'I love you, Gisela!'

Everyone could see it for miles around. I was touched, and my feelings said, 'yes!' On 13th August 1951, my mother's birthday, we became engaged. Now it was clear to everyone that we were a couple. Hamilton gave me a beautiful diamond ring which he had bought in Newquay.

Pictures from our trips to the coast together.

With Hamilton's help, I was able to take up my hobby of horse riding again. At Prideaux Place near Padstow, which I could reach by train from Wadebridge in those days, I hired a hack by the hour from a Mrs McBurnie. She would often accompany me as I rode the trail from Padstow to Harlyn Bay and back once a week so I could canter on the beach. Hamilton would pick me up in the car, because at the time there wasn't a train going back to Wadebridge.

Because Hamilton's work as a businessman meant he was very busy, he had a woman work for him as a home help, called Ruth Udy. She wanted to get married to her fiancé, Jack Mitchell, as soon as possible, and so wanted to give up her work. Hamilton had heard from Mr Vernon that I was a good worker, and that the same went for all German workers who decided to come to Britain – so Hamilton asked me whether I could recommend a young woman from my group of friends, who might want to leave Germany for work. I knew that my school friend Uschi Schacht would be interested, so I got in touch with her in Stralsund. She accepted the offer. Within a few weeks, she was in Wadebridge too. Hamilton paid for her passage, as Mr Vernon had done for me, and gave her a job. It was particularly important to Hamilton that I should maintain my old links with people at home in Stralsund. I sensed this attitude of his in other ways too; he tried to speak German, and to help me with the care packages that I continued to send back to Stralsund.

Now, of course, I went to Hamilton at Toll-Gate on my day off, which was always a Thursday. Before Ruth Udy left her job with Hamilton, I was able to get to know her better. We became very good friends and regularly visited each other. Ours was a friendship which would last until her death, more than sixty years later.

My relationship with Uschi Schacht, however, my German compatriot, could not be seen as a friendship exactly. She became hugely jealous of my relationship with Hamilton – she was always making advances on him, which was very embarrassing for me, because she knew we were engaged. One day, there was a dramatic scene in Toll-Gate, in which she managed to involve the whole household. I remember how she tried to take her own life in the flat at Toll-Gate, trying to cut her wrist – but, while it was dramatic, it wasn't life threatening. Once she had recovered, Hamilton found her work to go to in London. For now, the problem was solved. But the disappointment clung to me still, because I had recommended that she come here. But my connection to Uschi Schacht was not over in any sense – as would later become apparent.

In spite of all of this, my relationship with Hamilton didn't change. Now we began to plan our wedding, which was to take place that same year: we decided upon 24th November. Hamilton had a brother and four sisters, all of whom were older than him. His relationship with his siblings was not particularly close. Hamilton had not grown up in Newquay with his family, because his mother had died shortly after he was born. He had been brought up by his Aunt Bessy in Wadebridge, down on the Camel, on the Egloshayle

49

side of the town. The relationship between him and his brother was problematic, because he consistently refused to accept that a German woman would marry into the family. Hamilton was, at that time, a very successful businessman, and a popular and respected gentleman to boot – there was never any doubt in his mind that he would marry me.

But there still remained the issue of my commitment to going to Windhoek; I had already agreed with the German aid agency in Berlin that I would work there for a year. Hamilton and some of my other friends tried to talk me out of it. But it was a visit to a soothsayer in Harlyn Bay that decided it for me. She said that she foresaw in the stars that the trip would mean disaster for me. I didn't know whether I believed her, but it certainly made an impression on me. And so that was that. I changed my mind and stayed in Wadebridge, cancelling my commitment to the organisation.

An aerial view of Wadebridge.
Courtesy of ©Adrian Langdon.

My upcoming wedding also meant, of course, that I would no longer be working for the Vernon's on the farm. Because I had been hired to work for a year, and that year was not yet up, Hamilton paid Mr Vernon a sum of money which corresponded to the amount of time I had left on my contract, as 'investment'. And so the year had ended in quite a different way to the one I had anticipated. How could I have predicted this twelve months previously? Now I could concentrate properly on my commitment to Hamilton.

But I still asked myself over and over again, 'what am I doing? Am I doing the right thing?' I had to think of Aunt Frieda and Uncle Hermann in all of this, too, and what they'd say about it. I wasn't completely free of doubt, therefore, because I couldn't seek advice from any of my family. But my desire to live, and my positive experiences up until that point, far away from home, ultimately made my decision for me.

Although I hadn't fulfilled my whole years' service, the Vernons' goodbye to me was not unfriendly; Mr Vernon's business relationship with my future husband remained intact.

A Family of My Own

We were married on 24th November 1951, in the Methodist church on the eastern side of the river, right next to the bridge. Mr Vernon very kindly took on the role of father-of-the-bride, because of course nobody from my side of the family could do the job. A few members of Hamilton's family were present, including his brother and sister-in-law. Our reception was hosted at a café on Molesworth Street, and we had invited many of Hamilton's friends and business acquaintances to celebrate with us. I had mixed feelings in that moment; now I had a husband who loved me, who gave me strength and confidence, but also freedom and security. On the other hand, though, I was quite sad that I had no family to celebrate with me. My thoughts returned again to Aunt Frieda and Uncle Hermann.

Hamilton and I at our wedding.

Following the wedding, naturally I moved to Toll-Gate with Hamilton, where we would both live and work. The house was big enough to give a family plenty of room to live, and it was convenient, too, to have our workplace so close at hand. And so work and our home life got along together very well. Hamilton told me about the building's origins. He had bought the land before the war, in order to build a petrol station on it with service facilities for cars. He managed to do this with money borrowed from his brother Garfield, who was many years older than he was. Garfield already had just such a business in Newquay, and was doing very well from it. But then the war interrupted it all. Hamilton had to take up civil duties, important to the war, in a nearby foundry on Polmorla Road, making materials for the war effort. But afterwards, he returned to Toll-Gate, and actually it became a very successful venture.

For me, this was the start of a new life, full of hope. I knew that Hamilton always worked hard, and expected just as much from me. But that was in fact exactly what I wanted. I learnt a lot about the business, the petrol station, the shop – I served the customers and was pleased when they were happy.

Our first home together.

As was customary at that time, our honeymoon began immediately after the wedding. I wanted to go to London, because I wanted to get to know the city. We made the journey, and Hamilton showed me all the important sights. Now I was not just an honorary Englishwoman – I really began to feel it, too. Over time, I became so familiar with the culture, the language, the funny little customs, that I completely discarded the distance that I had kept earlier, as a German who had only been in this country a little while. When it came to pure Britishness, I felt like a part of society. I took on the Cornish patriotism, too, because it wasn't just about regional pride, but encompassed its own language, its own flag and hymns, and cultural specialities as well. Cornish miners are famous the world over, thanks to their extraordinary skill.

But Hamilton set great store by my links to my home country, and was determined that I shouldn't break them off. He sensed that the roots I still had were important to me. I told him that I wanted him to meet Aunt Frieda and Uncle Hermann; they had said in their letters that they were very proud that I had married an Englishman. Hamilton himself also wanted to get to know my relatives and the country I came from. So we planned to travel to Stralsund as soon as possible. We didn't do so lightly, though, because, after all, I had left East Germany illegally. I knew from the news and from my letters that those who made attempts to flee were being persecuted there - as soon as the authorities could get hold of them, they were arrested and sent to prison. Because of my marriage to Hamilton I now held a British passport. With this I could count on the fact that I would be allowed to enter the country and, more importantly, that I would be allowed to leave again. We agreed to make the trip to Germany as soon as we could.

But first, in 1952, we were joined by the patter of tiny feet – I was pregnant, and so excited to meet my first child. Hamilton was very pleased; it was his great wish to have children of his own. And so we began to organise our home for the arrival of our baby.

Peter came into this little world of ours on 15th September 1952. Mother and baby were fine and well, and so was his father, of course. From then on, the work at home and in the business came second to my baby son, as I took care of him as well.

As the owners of a private business, our work went on without a break. But the business was going well, and we could afford a few luxuries; driving through the countryside around Wadebridge brought me close to the beautiful landscape. From Land's End to Boscastle, Penzance to Truro, and Bodmin or Newquay to Padstow, I gradually came to know the Cornish people and places. As I have already mentioned, Hamilton's family lived in Newquay, but we rarely visited his brother, although we maintained a good contact with his sisters.

Incidentally, some of Hamilton's relatives lived and still live in New Zealand, where some of the Hawkey ancestors had emigrated. Many years later, I visited them there.

Despite being a busy mother I didn't forget about the connection to my friends and relatives in East Germany, though, particularly those in Stralsund. I wrote to them each year on birthdays and at Christmas, or sent packages and calendars with beautiful photographs of the Cornish coast, and they told me that they treasured everything I sent. I was always very excited to receive cards and letters from them. I enjoyed writing letters myself, using a little typewriter to write them out. That typewriter served me well over the years, and, although it doesn't work properly any more, I've still kept it. It wasn't possible to telephone all of my friends and relatives, as only certain people in East Germany had access to telephones, but I could speak to some of them this way. My friend Anneliese Friedrichs, for example, who kept a shop in Stralsund, on Heilgeist Strasse, had a telephone. In comparison to how easy it is now, calling somebody in those days was quite complicated; you could only do it by booking in advance with the telegraph office. And the East German state secret police, the Stasi, were probably listening in, too.

But in spite of that, we set our plans in motion. Our first journey was to West Berlin in 1954, where we met up with family and friends – including Aunt Frieda and Uncle Hermann. For this first trip we left Peter with Ruth Mitchell (nee Udy) in her cottage at St Breock. We were cautious, and didn't travel to the East straight away. It was safer for us that we met in West Berlin, close to the East German border. Hamilton paid to host our guests in a hotel in Zehlendorf, in the south-eastern outskirts of the city, near the Free

University, because they couldn't afford it themselves. I was thrilled to see familiar faces, after all the change I had been through; it had been a good three years since I left Stralsund.

L to R – Uncle Hermann, Aunt Liesbeth, Peter and Aunt Frieda in Lübeck.

In September 1955, when I was expecting our second child, we went to stay in Lübeck, a town in West Germany, not far from Hamburg and nearest the northern part of the border with the East. We had brought our son Peter with us. Aunt Frieda and Uncle Hermann came, bringing two more relatives with them from Stralsund, so that we could get to know each other as a family, including its new additions, enjoying – for a few days at least - the feeling that we all belonged together. We could share with everyone else the joy we felt at our impending arrival. We listened to the news and stories friends and relatives had to tell. We spent a few very happy days there, and then we dispersed, each travelling home with a sense of uncertainty. When would we see each other again? Creating this barrier, dividing people, splitting not just what had been our homeland but the entire continent into two blocs: the GDR certainly made its mark on my relationship with my family and friends in Germany.

It was on 28th March 1956 that Bruce, our second son, was born at Toll-Gate. Hamilton, Peter and I were of course overjoyed – now we were a family of four. I began to concentrate my efforts on the children and keeping the house, trying to make our home nice, arranging it so that it was cosy yet practical. The business kept Hamilton occupied, but at evenings and weekends he spent a lot of time with the children. We wanted to make sure that both of them would learn how to take control of their own lives, and be independent, and at four years old, they each began their education. First Peter and then Bruce started school in Wadebridge, on Lansdowne Road, a street that would later have another meaning for us. We continued to plan their education, and chose private schools for both of them.

After Bruce was born, Hamilton considered scaling back his work; the few problems he had with his health were his main reason for making his decision, or at least for being advised to do so. Using his business contacts, he was able to plan and effect two crucial changes for us.

In 1958, the petrol station and its land had all been sold to the fuel company Esso. We relocated to West Hill in Wadebridge, to a bungalow with a large garden. The little property was called Penwarne, and it would be our home for many years.

The proceeds from the sale of Toll Gate meant that Hamilton was able to buy a business premise in the centre of Wadebridge, on The Platt – he called it 'Hamilton House'. From then on, this building would be where both he and I worked, and so we opened our shop, which sold sweets, tobacco, ice cream, and more of the same sort of thing on one side, and fruit, vegetables, and other foods on the other. The shop was a success, which pleased us enormously; in fact, it went so well that we had to employ staff to help us. He used the railway link to London, which was still connected to Wadebridge by train in those days, to order fresh products to be sent to us. I can still remember the orders arriving at the shop from the nearby station, just after a train had pulled in. We also used the rail link to send fresh cream to London in tins.

Bit by bit, Hamilton fitted out the building and modernised its fixtures and fittings. The other shops were already let to tenants, like Mr Williams, the chemist, Barnecutts bakers, Howard & Tregunna Ltd, electrical retailers, and Eddy, the butcher. On the large, open-plan top floor, which was a furniture store, he constructed a mezzanine level and made nine offices which are still in use today.

(L) Our shop display. (R) Our rotating window display.

Our family, 1957.

I always kept items from my old German hometown in our house in Wadebridge, whether that meant things like pictures hanging on the wall, or table decorations. Following our trips to Germany, I always brought something back, and sometimes my relatives sent things to us. I particularly liked pictures of Stralsund and the surrounding coastline, like the island of Hiddensee. I was glad to be as close to the water in Cornwall as I had been in Stralsund. I visited the sea just as often in my new home. If the weather was good, we often liked to take the children to Constantine Bay, because the sand dunes there reminded me of the Baltic coast, and because they were perfect for the children to play in. In those days, it was easy to drive there and to park the car – but today so many drivers visit these beaches that sometimes you can't find a space. And it's not free any more, either, like it was then.

Happy days at Constantine Bay.

One day, we heard from Mr Vernon the farmer that he had no use for his sheepdog any more, and was going to give him away. And so we came to be the owners of an Alsatian called Storm, who Hamilton came to love after a while. He had been a RAF police dog, and so he was very observant, constantly watching. He always did as Hamilton told him. At Toll-Gate, he'd lie at the bottom of the stairs all night, guarding us.

(L) Storm, our Alsatian, Hamilton's shadow. (R) Storm riding on the car boot.

Our two boys took great delight in him. But his end was sad; now and then he'd go to the abattoir nearby, to scavenge for a bone, but on one occasion he was beaten so badly by one of the men who worked there, that he returned home whimpering and badly hurt. He died shortly afterwards.

Some older residents of Wadebridge still remember Storm. Hamilton had a car with a 'fold down' boot lid. Storm would ride around the town standing on the lid, much to local amusement.

Among the many friends and business acquaintances Hamilton knew was a Mr Everett, from Reading. He lived in a house with a big plot of land right on the river, to the north of Wadebridge. The property was called Tregonce Cliff, and it had originally been arable land. Mr Everett lived quite a reclusive life, really, but he was very close to Hamilton and would often invite us and our friends onto his land. We enjoyed being there, especially in the summer months, because there was enough space to spend the whole day wandering around outside, to have barbecues, play games, or go bathing. The season usually began at Easter, with bathing in the river itself, or in a pool that was embedded in the rock and topped up by the river. For the children, it was absolute paradise, and both of the boys learnt to swim there. Our many visits to Mr Everett's estate and the happy hours we spent there became part of family life.

I made many more journeys to Stralsund, with Hamilton and with the boys, taking one of them each time. We still met up with friends and relatives – we always had so much to tell each other, because the separation of East and West affected all our communication. But, because of the political situation, we had to be very careful not to put anybody in danger. As we were visitors from a foreign, capitalist country, as far as the East German authorities were concerned, we were without doubt under observation at all times, but we used the visits to catch up with the people I knew all the same. And so my faraway home stayed close to me, and, as I'd hoped, it became my family's home too; Hamilton got to know my friends, my relatives, and my homeland. We went swimming together on the Baltic coast, which was so familiar to me because of the times I had made trips there in the past. For Hamilton, though, this was a truly unknown world.

Visiting East Germany.

We didn't just travel to the East, however – we also wanted to visit towns and cities in West Germany, like when we took Peter on a trip to Munich. He must have been around five years old at the time. We visited the zoo, among other things, and watched the zookeepers feeding the elephants. At that time, health and safety standards weren't quite what they are today; at any rate, I saw one of the elephants pick up Peter with its trunk, and set him down again in its enclosure. Onlookers screamed, of course, and the keepers had to retrieve my little boy, but not before the elephant emptied the entire contents of his trunk all over him. I certainly shan't forget that episode in a hurry – Peter survived it unscathed.

These trips, though, were only one part of our family life. Daily chores took up most of our time together, as they do in any family with small children. But we thrived on our busy yet quiet existence. I had found a place where I could work and care for my family, providing them with a safe and happy childhood, as my parents and earlier generations of my family had done for me.

Peter riding the elephant in Munich.

When both of the boys were old enough, they began to bring friends home. They had spent many happy hours at both Toll-Gate and Penwarne. They had their games and their high jinks, as all children do, and they never had any problems at school or in their personal development.

Gardening was what I did to relax at home. It gave me time to reflect. Caring for the plants, then watching them grow and bloom, was like communicating directly with nature. When my efforts were no longer enough, or when I struggled to grow something, I always found people to help me – but I have always felt a joy in having my own garden.

Another Disaster

Our family life continued as normal for the most part. The shop took priority for Hamilton, while I mainly looked after the two boys and the housework. Peter, our eldest son, was ten, and Bruce was three days short of his seventh birthday. Both were at school during the day. There were of course little problems day to day, which arise in any family, but these were manageable. And so our situation, after eleven years with Hamilton, would suddenly be turned on its head without warning.

Hamilton House, pictured in the 1980's.

On 25th March 1963, a day like any other, Hamilton was at work in our shop. I knew his daily routine: at seven o'clock in the evening, he would close the shop, balance the till, and return home. That meant that he would ride his little motorbike along the short distance of The Platt, up to West Hill, to where we lived at Penwarne. I always expected him at around eight o'clock. On this particular day, I was busy preparing for a small party we were having for Bruce, whose birthday we were to celebrate a few days later. Everything was as it normally was.

But, instead of Hamilton walking through the front door, the doorbell suddenly began to ring. Hingston Wood, a local farmer and friend, stood on the step, and he had terrible news for me.

"Mrs Hawkey, come quickly – Mr Hawkey is lying in the street, he must have had an accident!"

How had this happened? At this stage no one knew. The children were already asleep. I ran out with Mr Wood, and saw Hamilton lying there at the side of the road in the rain, bleeding. His words were barely audible.

"Help me, help me, help me."

His motorbike lay somewhere on the other side of the road – I could only see my husband, only wanted to help him. In the meantime, somebody had rung for help, and an ambulance arrived shortly afterwards. They picked up Hamilton and loaded him into the ambulance. I went with him, while a neighbour stayed behind with the children. We were taken to the hospital in Truro; I held Hamilton's hand on the journey, noticing that his vital signs were growing weaker. He became colder, and his cry for help even quieter. I saw the blood coming from his nose and his ears. I feared that he wouldn't survive the journey.

"He's dying, he is dying!" I cried, as a nurse who was accompanying us tried to comfort me.

I did not want it to be true – for another person I loved to have to leave me. When we arrived at the hospital, they knew already that we were coming in, and a surgeon named Mr Rutter was to take care of Hamilton. He was taken out of the ambulance and I was led to a separate room. After some time, a nurse came to me and tried to offer me a cup of tea – I recognised this gesture immediately as a warning sign.

"No," I refused, *"I want to see my husband!"*

I jumped up and wanted to go to Hamilton immediately. The nurse couldn't stop me, and eventually took me to see the doctor. I demanded of him too, to let me see my husband.

"I'm very sorry," he said, though, *"I've seen your husband. I'm afraid there was nothing we could do for him – he has died."*

I didn't want to believe it. I wanted to see Hamilton immediately. Somebody took me to him, and I saw that he was still wearing his clothes. They hadn't even been able to operate on him – he must have died while he was in the ambulance. And all the while I had been holding his hand. In that moment, my worst fear came true. The doctor explained Hamilton's injuries to me; they had been severe – fatal.

The ambulance took me home again. My thoughts and feelings tumbled around inside my head. Within just a few hours, my whole world had been destroyed again. I contemplated suicide – I thought that I wouldn't be able to bear life without him. But my children, waiting for me at home, stopped me going through with it.

When I arrived back at home, Hamilton's brother from Newquay was waiting there, as was one of his sisters. I had no good news to give them. The following day, a friend of mine, Ruth Menhinick, came and spent a few days with me and the children. She was German too, born Ruth Schäfer, and lived on Burniere Farm, north of Wadebridge. We are still good friends to this day.

Hamilton's relatives and friends – particularly a cousin Nesta Henwood and her husband Frank, who lived in Wadebridge – helped me to withstand the days that followed. Somebody still had to run the shop, because our income depended on it, and the children had to be looked after, and, after a few days, they had to be taken back to school. During that time, I just tried to function and keep life going as normal, although I found it very hard. Their father's death had upset the boys a great deal. Bruce was very sad, but he seemed to come around to the situation quite quickly, probably because he was so very young. But Peter was in complete shock. He refused to go to school, and stayed in bed all day. He had had a difficult time in his life already – we had removed him from his boarding school in Truro fairly recently, because of a falling out with a teacher. And now, to top it all, he had lost his father too.

In spite of all this, life went on. But, to me, time stood still. How was I supposed to go on after this catastrophe? For the second time in my life, fate dropped me into the depths of an abyss, the scale of which I couldn't comprehend.

In one of life's cruel ironies, my husband's will lay on the table the very day he died, waiting for his signature. We had spoken during the day and agreed he would not be home late as he wanted to read and sign it. The fact that it was never signed created a host of legal hurdles later in sorting out his affairs.

Back in Niepars in 1945, when by chance I was the only one of my family to escape death, strangers had nursed me back to health – brought me back to life – which was no longer the life I knew, or in fact wanted. But I had learnt to accept it, to carry on living in spite of my grief for the ones I had lost. Back then, I had been fighting for myself – I had to fight to survive in the weeks and the years that followed. From my experience in 1945, I knew that, given time, the inner pain I felt would diminish. But the soul itself carries that injury forever.

Very soon after the accident, I think perhaps a day or so later, the police clarified the course of events. A call was put out on local radio on the same day, in a search for witnesses to the accident and, if possible, the person who had caused it. A local farmer heard the plea, and immediately made the connection between what had happened the previous evening and a damaged car he had found abandoned in a ditch on the edge of his field. The driver of the car had appeared at his house that evening, asking to use his telephone. He let her, of course, because she said that she had driven her car into a ditch, and so she wanted to call her husband. The farmer had been struck immediately by how drunk the woman was. But first thing the next morning, after hearing the broadcast on local radio, he had put two and two together, making the connection with Hamilton's accident. Suspicious, he had informed the police. It came to light that the woman had drunk so much in a pub, down on The Platt in Wadebridge that the landlord had sent her on her way – to drive herself home. That had sealed Hamilton's fate, because she had taken the same route as him, driving close behind him. At the crossing of West Hill Road, where Hamilton would turn left towards Penwarne and so had to brake, the driver had raced at high speed – probably without being able to see a thing, as it was dark and raining – ramming into his motorcycle from behind. She drove away from the scene, leaving Hamilton lying there, seriously injured.

The legal struggle between us and the woman who had caused Hamilton's death lasted around three years, until it finally delivered a sentence; the case even went as far as the Royal Courts of Justice in London.

Her punishment for this was relatively lenient. She would be banned from driving for seven years and was ordered to pay damages of some £5,750.00, nominally for my children's school fees. Although I knew that she lived on the north coast of Cornwall, I never saw her again.

Hamilton's grave in Wadebridge on the 53rd Anniversary of his death in 2016 - it was at the insistence of Mr Everett, of Tregonce Cliff, where we had spent so many happy days, that the epitaph 'Nature's Perfect Gentleman' was placed on the gravestone.

I was much too young to be widowed, and could only numb my soul by throwing myself into work, which I had to do, because life had to go on, in spite of everything that had happened. Hamilton House was my work – it had been my husband's project, and I wanted to preserve it so that one day my children could take it over. I knew that Hamilton had built up his career as a businessman from nothing, beginning by eking out a living with borrowed money. But his years of work had been successful, and everybody in the area knew Mr Hawkey. His work had made him a prosperous businessman and given him a good reputation. Now it fell to me to carry on his legacy.

A Life for My Children

With Hamilton's death our lives changed overnight. I hadn't just lost my husband and the father of my children, but a devoted man of business, who secured the existence of our enterprise and its employees. Now his work and responsibility rested solely on my shoulders. Had I been alone, I would have pulled the plug on it all. But I couldn't just think of myself. Hamilton's wish and the ultimate aim of his endeavours was that our children's future should be secured through our work together, namely that of Hamilton House. And so I threw myself into work there. All our employees stood by my side; without them I wouldn't have been able to manage. The work served to conceal all of the wrangling, quarrelling emotions and thoughts I had about my fate, just as it had back in the years that followed 1945. Given that I had lost Hamilton, and our two boys had lost their father, I wanted to be there for both of them.

Before Hamilton's death, a range of choices had been open to us with regard to their education. We had earmarked private schools for both boys, conveniently located establishments, and with good reputations. From 1960 until 1962, Peter was a pupil at Treliske School, a boarding school in Truro. However, things didn't turn out very well. One particular teacher at this school made Peter's life difficult – why, we have never been able to fathom. But it was such that Hamilton, with the help of a Conservative MP, Scott-Hopkins, made a complaint against this teacher. We had already removed Peter from the school and brought him back to Wadebridge, to attend a local school there, Gonvena House School. This was followed suddenly by Hamilton's death, and so after that Peter had to adjust to another place and perspective.

After Hamilton died, Peter was little more than ten years old, and Bruce was nearing his seventh birthday. I was showered with so many questions about how I was going to manage to be both a mother from then on and to run a business at the same time. After their father's shocking death, both boys were of course traumatised. We lived through some dark days. But life had to go on. Eventually, both of the boys were able to return to school, and get used to the new situation.

That's what I had to do, too. The main question I had to answer was that of the boys' future education. Hamilton and I had made clear plans in this regard, and I didn't want to deviate from them. But how could I make these plans a reality now, all by myself? With my obligation to pay death duties on Hamilton's estate still to be finalised, and likely to be substantial, what could I afford? The Rev and Mrs Watts, the head teachers of Gonvena House, helped me, suggesting that I enquire at a private school near London, which was set up mainly for children who had lost one or both parents. Fees would be adjusted according to the parent's means. This boarding school was called Reeds School, and it was in Cobham, Surrey, southwest of London. The school agreed to take them and the paying of fees was later helped by the award of damages against the woman who had caused Hamilton's death.

Peter started at Reeds School in September 1964, after two years at Gonvena School. Due to his September birthday, he was one of the oldest in his year. Perhaps this was an advantage, though, and helped him to settle in. He left the school after seven years, in 1971

Bruce followed Peter to Reeds in 1967, having been a pupil at the same Wadebridge school from 1962. I'd like to mention that, each year, the Queen would nominate two of the school's new pupils, to be educated there. This was a purely honorary award from Her Majesty, as patron of the school. When Bruce began his education there, he was chosen to receive the honour. I felt very proud and grateful.

In hindsight, I can absolutely say for both of my children that they had a very good education. Because they were away from home, I wasn't able to give them my personal attention and devotion, which was difficult for me, of course. But it was a compromise that I had to make, because I was as good as exhausted by the work at Hamilton House. I made several trips a year to London, obviously, to see the boys, and I wrote them letters, and we spoke on the telephone. The distance from Cornwall to London meant that the children were not able to travel home at half-term, or on other occasions like bank holidays. At such times, they would stay with the parents of school friends or other family friends in the London area. At the end of the school term, they would return with their large school trunk, as was usual at the time, travelling by train to Wadebridge. During these holidays they nurtured local friendships and hobbies. John, the son of Ruth Mitchell, who had always helped at Toll-Gate, was a great friend of the boys. It is a friendship which still continues on today.

Her Majesty
The Queen
is pleased to nominate
Bruce Holger Hawkey
for education at
Reed's School

15th September, 1967

Queen's Nomination.

As was typical at boarding school, much of the boys' free time was given over to sport. Reeds taught and played rugby, of course, along with hockey, and that most English of pursuits, cricket. Both of the boys represented the school, Peter with perhaps more success. As it turned out, his sportiness would come into play in his future job too.

I followed in Hamilton's footsteps with Hamilton House and the business, organising the products and arranging deliveries, making sales, dealing with the bank, drawing up contracts and settling accounts – everything that was necessary to keep the business running as it should. That was important to me.

BUCKINGHAM PALACE

9th October, 1967.

Dear Mrs Hawkey,

I am commanded by The Queen to thank
you very much indeed for your letter of 27th
September thanking Her Majesty for the nomination
of your son to Reed's School, Cobham, Surrey.

The Queen hopes that your son will
spend successful and enjoyable years at Reed's
School.

Yours sincerely,

Philip Moon

Mrs Gisela Hawkey.

Reply from Buckingham Palace.

Bruce (left) and Peter (right) in London during their school days.

I watched my boys grow up with pride and happiness. They both passed their school exams, and therefore had the qualifications to go on to further study. I had no doubt that both would find their way in life and could handle anything. Hamilton would have loved to see them too. I never needed to convince or persuade the boys to do anything – they knew in their hearts exactly what they wanted to do.

During the summer before leaving school, Peter stayed with friends in Hamburg. They had secured him a job at the docks as a Gastarbeiter, a casual worker. He was the only Englishman there, working mainly with Turks, from whom he started to learn German.

Having left school, Peter took a year off. He had secured a place to study Physical Education and Geography at St Luke's College Exeter, now a part of the University of Exeter; the college agreed to allow him a gap year, and to defer his place to the following year. Much of this year was spent living in Rotterdam, doing unpaid voluntary work for the Mission to Seamen. I like to think that his payment was a practical way of learning about real life.

Bruce left the school in 1974. Straightaway he moved on to study mechanical engineering at Rycotewood College in Thame, near Oxford. He later went on to secure a job with John Deere in Nottingham, specialists in agricultural machinery, working there from 1980 until 1982, before continuing his career with them in Australia.

At the beginning of the 1980s, I therefore had two grown-up sons, who had completed their education and were paying their own way in the world; I had seen to it that this part of Hamilton's wish had been fulfilled, and so I was grateful and happy.

Peter (left) and Bruce (right) at Reeds School in 1975.

At the same time, I had successfully preserved Hamilton House, as it was generally known. During the preceding years, Cornwall had become more and more attractive to tourists, which was a boon for local people and their economy. Many tourists later settled in second homes in our county. Set against this backdrop, I could busy myself with Hamilton's work.

As time went by, physical work began to cause me problems. In 1968, my doctor had found a swelling in my abdomen, and he advised me to have an operation. For a time, I lived in fear of having cancer, but luckily the tumour was benign. In spite of this, on the doctor's advice I decided to have a hysterectomy. But after that I made an obvious mistake. I returned to the shop too soon, and worked too hard carrying fruit crates. The result was a bladder prolapse, and I had to go under the knife once more, with the operation taking place this time at a London clinic. Afterwards, I had to give up the physical work in the shop, and so I let out the shop at Hamilton House to a very kind couple, taking on the role of landlady. In doing so, I had gained more time for myself, which I could use to travel, among other things.

Disappointment

I want to take you back a little in time again to the 1950's and early1960's. I want to relate another story which the boys and I have often discussed over the years and will always be a disappointing memory to us all. Following Hamilton's death and after some time the boy's started to settle into their school routines. I was hoping things would begin to go smoothly.

Mr Everett, Hamilton's great friend, was a widower and significantly older than him. Their friendship blossomed through a mutual interest in investment and the more technical aspects of property development.

In around 1950, Mr Everett had purchased the property, Tregonce Cliff, which sat on the banks of the River Camel. The view of the surrounding landscape is simply breath-taking – you can look directly out to the mouth of the river. On the left-hand side lies Padstow, with its little harbour basin, and on the right the picturesque village of Rock.

Behind the property lies what is today known as the Camel Trail, a popular cycle path from Bodmin to Padstow following the route of the old railway line. In those days, the trains would go past at regular intervals, steaming and whistling. So often did we visit, and so happy were those times, that Tregonce felt as though it had become a piece of our home.

Mr Everett's friendship meant that, in our free time, mostly on Sundays or Bank Holidays, that we would pack up a picnic and both of the children, and take them to Tregonce. The children could play and rampage through the extensive grounds. It was a little idyll complete with one dog, 'Dash', and two small ponies, one by the name of 'Duchess'. Hamilton always helped his friend with various maintenance issues around the property. In the summer, the boys would often camp there in their tent, or stay in one of the three caravans on the site.

Tregonce Cliff, with its natural swimming pool.

I noticed that Mr Everett approached my husband in such a trusting, confident way, that it was as if Hamilton were his son. I was obviously not wrong about that, because one day Mr Everett invited Hamilton to visit, but without the rest of the family. When he returned home, he told me straightaway why Mr Everett had asked him to go; he had opened up to Hamilton, telling him that he was ill with cancer, his health was failing and he had perhaps just a few years left to live. And so he intended to bequeath his local estate to our family, because he had no children of his own. Only a sister-in-law and her husband, Captain Hawkes, should own the land if they were to outlive him. After that, as he foresaw it, it would be our property. And so it was finally legally certified. We were quite touched by all this, and couldn't comprehend it straightaway. Now our bond with Mr Everett had grown still deeper. Although we now knew of his illness, we didn't let on, and the visits and camping on his grounds went on as it had done before. We felt happiest there, and spent many joy-filled hours and days together, happy about our prospects for the future, particularly when we thought of our boys. At that time, we still lived and worked at Toll-Gate, the petrol station, which housed the shop and our flat.

Running the petrol station meant that, especially in the summer months, we came into contact with many tourists, who would travel to our beautiful part of the world for some rest and relaxation, and we had one or two friendly exchanges with them. One day Hamilton alerted me to a married couple whose car was being filled. He called to me, telling me that I ought to come over for a moment, because he recognised the woman to be German. And so we got talking. My former homeland was always an interesting topic for me. That's how we got to know Ingrid and Arthur Matthews (names changed). It was around the late 1950s that we first met. They came from Reading, and were on their way to a bed and breakfast in Cornwall. We found them to be a friendly couple, and agreed to meet them the following Sunday to have lunch together. Because we also had a date with Mr Everett on that particular Sunday, I asked him whether he would mind us bringing the Matthews with us. Mr Everett was very much an introverted soul, but he agreed happily. And thus came about the connection between Mr Everett and the Matthews, whose daughter was around the same age as Peter.

In the time that followed, our relationship with Ingrid and Arthur grew closer, and we became firm friends. You could say that we knew each other very well. Ingrid and I talked a lot about our earlier lives in Germany. Arthur Matthews was a successful mechanic. In one moment of confidence, I told them of Mr Everett's decision to leave Tregonce Cliff to us in his will – that was a mistake, but I only recognised it as such much later on. A few years passed, and Hamilton was killed. Mr Everett had lost a true friend in him, and was grief-stricken. You will recall that it was he who insisted upon the epitaph 'nature's perfect gentleman' on Hamilton's gravestone. After the funeral he tried to reassure and comfort me.

"Don't worry, Gisela," he said, "Tregonce is still for you and the boys." He also wanted to know when I would conclude the arrangements we had agreed with regard to Tregonce Cliff. I told him that I'd confirm it with him, because it was the obvious thing to do, in the interest of my two children. The documents were signed and sealed in late 1963.

Mr Everett became more and more afflicted by his illness. He had to be taken to a clinic in Reading to be treated there. His treatment lasted a long while and, in that time, I didn't see him at all. The illness had obviously become such that he wasn't able to travel back to Cornwall. And so it was that Mr Everett died of cancer in the clinic. His last will and testament came into effect, and his sister-in-law took over the land as its new owner. This is what had been planned, as I was well aware. I sometimes met Captain and Mrs Hawkes in Wadebridge when they were staying at Tregonce Cliff. They were very kind and, like Mr Everett, rather old. I knew them from earlier visits to the estate, because they had visited too when Mr Everett had been alive. But, to my utmost horror, I learnt from them that Mr Everett's will had been changed once more while he had been in Reading, completely unbeknown to me.

When I enquired further, I found out that it was not our family but the Matthews who had been named in Mr Everett's will as the next owners of Tregonce Cliff – our supposed friends, who had only been introduced to the man and found out his intentions with regard to his property through us. I felt that the rug had been pulled from beneath my feet – I didn't want to believe it. For now, Captain Hawkes and his wife were the owners of the land in any case, but, up until this moment, I had assumed that at some point in the not-too-distant future, my children and I would live there. This unexpected disappointment, that Peter and Bruce felt too, of course, was admittedly not life-threatening, but once again misfortune had crept up on me when I had least expected it.

Why Mr Everett altered his will in favour of the Matthews, without telling me anything about it, I had no idea. He was seriously ill, and, as I learnt from Captain Hawkes, Ingrid Matthews, who had apparently been my friend, had courted Mr Everett in a way – ingratiating herself with frequent visits. But I couldn't help thinking that all this had only been an effort to change his will, to our disadvantage. Even if it had been out of special gratitude to Ingrid Matthews, I still ought to have been privy to the information; that would be my understanding of friendship in such circumstances, at any rate. Furthermore, such was the bond between Mr Everett and Hamilton that I have little doubt that this is not how he would act in normal circumstances. Ingrid Matthews tried to come and see me one more time, but I would not let her in, and showed her the door – she had betrayed me as a friend.

Ironically, the Matthews rarely visited the property, and it fell into decline and decay; perhaps guilt over how they had acquired Tregonce meant that they never really felt comfortable there. After some years, in yet another twist of fate, the property was acquired by a man called Nigel Middleton, who had been a school friend from Reeds School, and now had a dental practise in the town. Such a strange coincidence, but now the property was, at least, loved as a home again.

Tregonce Cliff would later change hands, at higher and higher prices, today valued in the millions. But to us, it was lost. And the people we had thought to be our friends – well, they turned out to be no such thing. I'd had to live through much worse things, it's true, but why must I so often be on the receiving end of these things?

On the Move

My two sons, now grown up, educated and at work, decided in the early 1980s to forge their own paths, to live and work all over the free world. They were made tempting proposals, and what young person doesn't long to travel? They had other motives too, though. Wadebridge, their little hometown, would always be associated with Hamilton, their father; Tregonce Cliff too, that children's paradise on the banks of the River Camel, where they had spent so many happy hours was taken away from us. Perhaps the strong emotional connection to what had always been their home was somehow diminished. The fact that both boys spent years at a boarding school may also have played a part. After leaving school, they both went away to college and, by the end of their education, both had learned to be independent. They did not have the same network of local family or friends that many other children had, and had no fear of making their own way in the world.

What had happened to me between 1945 and 1951 in my own homeland was of course quite different, but inside I could see the similarities. My feelings were therefore at odds with one another. Hamilton House, their father's physical legacy, demanded all my strength and energy, especially in the early days. But something always came up that I couldn't manage on my own. On the other hand, I knew from my own experience that such life changing opportunities like these, to move away and travel the world, were a strong force which put everything into perspective. And so the boys went their separate ways, and they were with me in my thoughts as I kept their home. Unlike me, they could return home whenever they liked.

In 1981, after 5 years of teaching at Stonyhurst College in Lancashire, Peter went to teach at Aiglon College in Switzerland, a private international school where young, privileged children from around the world were educated. He taught sports there until 1991. As part of his work there, he made many trips abroad with his pupils, including to Mount Kilimanjaro. After ten years at the school, though, he was ready for a change. In September 1991 he left the school and became involved in the ski business, working at a specialist shop for skiwear and equipment. Obviously this meant that he was most busy during the winter ski season, and therefore he had part of the year left over to use for travel around the world. Australia, New Zealand and the US were among the countries he wanted to visit, but also African countries too. Among other trips, he trekked the Annapurna Circuit for about three weeks. In the summers of 1996 and 1997, Peter re-trained as a sports therapist. In 1998, he settled in Wadebridge and started his sports therapy business.

Peter in the Swiss Alps.

Visiting Bruce in Sydney.

Bruce, on the other hand, went straight to the other side of the world. His company, John Deere, offered him a position in Australia, where he worked from 1982 until 1986, with great success. In 1986 he made the decision to return home, and to do so by crewing on yachts. But, during the journey, while he was in Fiji, a call from the Japanese company Kubota reached him, offering him a significant job and package. That's how life goes sometimes. This offer was a good one, and so he accepted the position and stayed with Kubota for another sixteen years. He lived in Queensland, Brisbane, Sydney, and later in Melbourne, where he had responsibility for Kubota's Industrial Division performance across Australia, New Zealand and Papua New Guinea. He still enjoyed sailing both in Port Phillip Bay, Melbourne, and some ocean passages including Hawaii to Alaska, where he met Peter for a holiday. He came back to Wadebridge in July 2003.

Obviously I have always stayed in contact with both of my sons. I also knew that both of them were in constant touch with each other too. Therefore I could be content and proud. They had both, because of their jobs and their private travels, visited different continents in the world. Because at home all was running well at Hamilton House, I was able to visit both of my sons on several occasions. I often went to see Peter in Switzerland, and I flew to Australia to see Bruce five times, from there visiting New Zealand four times. I always began the journeys there two weeks before Christmas and stayed until February. My sons lived and worked in these countries, so I wasn't just given the tourist highlights – I experienced the everyday lives of the people in the area. At the same time, my visits were always prime opportunities to exchange family news. From all this I learnt a great deal about the way people lived, and their values, as well as being able to see quite different kinds of plants and animals to the ones I was used to at home. I became something of a world citizen, even if only in my own personal sense. I was so impressed by New Zealand and Australia that I could have lived there if circumstances had allowed.

I travelled within Europe and North Africa too, visiting different countries. I can vividly remember a three-week trip to Italy, as well as trips to Austria, Spain, and Morocco.

I wouldn't have gone behind the Iron Curtain, though, into East Germany, if that hadn't been my home, and if the many people who were so dear to me had no longer lived there. I was able to – or had to – watch how a grey veil lay over the country, in the truest sense of the words. Streets and whole towns were visibly decaying, and symptoms of deficiency shaped the lives of the people who lived there. The political powers and authorities claimed, however, that the opposite was happening – though only those who never saw it for themselves could believe it. It was particularly clear during my visits in the 1980s, when I travelled alone, that the dictators and ideologists couldn't make life any better for the people in the East than it was for those in the West, with free economies, freedom of thought, and human rights.

Every so often, my two boys would come back to Wadebridge, and so they never truly gave up their connection to their home. Each time they returned I was filled with joy, and sometimes I even waited for their advice.

At home in Cornwall.

They used their time at home to visit their friends, and to see Hamilton House too. On one such visit from Australia in 1991, I think, Bruce looked for some property in Wadebridge in order to move me closer to the town. Our old home, Penwarne, had many steps and a large garden, and had become too much for me to maintain, particularly with my arthritic knees. He went to an estate agent, Jeff Cole, whom we knew well, but they were unable to find a suitable property. The day before leaving to return to Australia Bruce went to the office to say goodbye and to thank him for his help. The agent asked if Bruce would be interested in a plot of land on Lansdowne Road, which had just come onto the market. They walked to the plot to take a look. Bruce didn't have to think for long. He discussed it with me and his brother Peter, and completed the deal a day after he had returned to Australia. Now began a building project, designed and planned between us, with me in Wadebridge, Peter in Switzerland, and Bruce in Melbourne. The plans travelled around the world many times. They consisted of two separate houses with gardens and garages. Bruce put his savings into the second house as an investment. And that's just what was built. In 1994 we moved into Hamilton Court in Lansdowne Road. It was our brand-new home. Just like Toll-Gate and Penwarne, it sat on the hillside in Wadebridge on the western bank of the Camel.

Our new home, Hamilton Court.

I still live here today, and I have kept faith in this part of the world since I first moved into Mr Vernon's farmhouse in 1951. I couldn't have predicted in any way that I'd end up living here. But, as I said, we Pomeranian folk put down firm roots. I'm a good example of that. Although I've made a great many trips around the world from this house, my steps always lead back to here. We applied for and obtained permission to call our new development 'Hamilton Court', which along with Hamilton House, our commercial building in the town, are a welcome memory of my husband who was so cruelly taken from us.

I should mention that we often laugh about the move to the new house. You will appreciate that moving house after many years is a big move, even if it is only 'down the road', and remember I was around seventy years old. Peter was able to help, but Bruce could not return from Australia. I enlisted the help of two dear German friends, Hanni Kuchnowski and Inge Krempin, both from Stralsund, who would help me in exchange for some time in Cornwall. Now, in our family we have opposites: I am a hoarder who keeps everything, as does Bruce, whilst Peter will quickly throw something out if he sees no need to keep it. With my two German friends it was exactly the same – Hanni thought like me, and Inge related exactly to Peter. The two natural teams went to work. Peter and Inge walking down the path to throw all manner of things in the rubbish bin, to be followed minutes later by me and Hanni to take it out and bring it back for packing. Peter is adamant the move could have been done in half the time if not for this battle.

Two worlds

My birthplace, my parents' house, my childhood, my youth –
everything was in Pomerania (though now it's part of the state
Mecklenburg-Vorpommern). After the war, it became part of East
Germany, the Soviet-occupied zone. In this part of Germany in the
years that followed, a Communist dictatorship developed, following
the model of the Soviet Union. Leaving to one side the post-war
emergency which plagued Germany and indeed the whole of
Europe, it was apparent by the end of 1949 that the two parts of
Germany were polarising, becoming absorbed into different, even
enemy power blocs. I appeared to be caught between the two, and
I doubted whether I was on the right side. We Pomeranian folk
are rooted to our soil, we like to stay in familiar territory – but I
had lost so much, namely my family, that I had to leave. I made my
decision, therefore, relatively quickly.

The link to my homeland has, however, influenced my entire
life. Having found a new place to live and build a new home, as I
had managed to do in Wadebridge, did not mean I could forget my
old life and home, and all that had passed before. In my thoughts
and in my deeds, I always remained linked to the place that had
been my home. Unfortunately, my old home now lay behind a
virtually insurmountable wall. I had to live in two worlds – there
was no other way about it.

Since leaving East Germany in 1951, it became clear to me
that I couldn't go back: not as long as the threat of persecution
remained, in any case, nor this disagreeable state of affairs. Later,
when I had my own family in Wadebridge, I no longer contemplated
the possibility of going back at all. And the political relationship
between the East and the West seemed to be cemented for the rest
of my life, so I did anything I could to maintain contact with my
friends and relatives in the GDR.

Through my marriage to Hamilton, though, I had become
a British citizen, and so I was able to travel to my former home
whenever I wished, though it was a long drawn out process to
get the required permits. You had to be careful, however, because

the East German constitution did not recognise individual human rights, as we do in the West. In 1954, Hamilton and I travelled initially to West Berlin, staying in Zehlendorf. There we stayed in a hotel with family and friends from Stralsund, who had dared to travel to the West. At this time, there was still no physical Berlin Wall. We were all of course overjoyed to see each other again, to have direct contact with one another for the first time since the so-called Iron Curtain went up.

Some years later – it must have been in about 1957 – we risked a trip to Stralsund. We drove in our car, an Austin, travelling with special fuel additives for it as a precaution against poor quality fuel, to keep the engine going. Hamilton as a mechanic would also take a selection of spare parts. Under no circumstances did we want to risk our car getting damaged during the journey through East Germany. We took our son Peter with us – he was four years old at the time, while Bruce was left at home with my good friend Ruth Mitchell.

The car was full of fresh fruit, like oranges and bananas, as well as chocolate and coffee; we knew that these items were much sought after by the people we were visiting. In the East there were very few goods like this, or perhaps none at all – that we already knew. The East German regime was desperate for foreign currency and had devised various means to get it. At the border, for example, you had to declare how many days you would stay in East Germany. You would then have to hand over a fee for every day in hard western currency. I forget the amount but it was significant and non-re-fundable. Then there were so-called Intershops, where foreign visitors could buy 'luxury goods', but only pay with western currency. I remember going to the Intershop at Rugendamm station to buy things for friends and relatives. These 'luxury goods' were not luxury as we understood it – just simple things that were not available in the East.

The journey at that time was very difficult, and we had to make many stops along the way. Border controls in the East were generally very unfriendly and the regime's claim to power left its mark on everyone, in particular of course on visitors from the so-called *Feindgebiet* – the outside world, on the Western side of the Iron Curtain – as far as they were concerned, it was enemy territory. Even though we came in peace, for purely humanitarian purposes, it made no difference. As soon as we arrived in Stralsund, the first stop was the police station, where we had to hand over our passports to be kept there until we were due to leave. This trip thankfully came to an uneventful end. Back in Lübeck, the closest West German city to the border, we took a deep breath. On all visits after that – because we did carry on going – there was this feeling of relief when we returned to the West, the relief at having returned to freedom. Besides, we had a feeling that, in East Germany, we were being kept under surveillance. They couldn't deceive us.

With Hamilton's death in 1963, our travels together stopped. In spite of that, over a period of about three or four years, I did some travelling of my own by train. On my journeys I often met up with those who I had left behind in the East in 1951, those who I knew from my time there. And the children of my friends and relatives too, who were born into this divided world. When we talked together it was always very intense, because everybody had so much to say to one another. Amongst other things, I was able to tell them what was going on in the West, on the other side of the Iron Curtain. Stories like mine, though true and honest information, were routinely repressed by the regime.

In any case, my closest friends and relatives knew everything that had happened to me up until the point where I fled East Germany – so some of them also knew that, on 1st May 1945, a Georgian doctor serving in the Red Army had saved me from death, having brought me back to life after my suicide attempt. This doctor's name was Temo Melikidse. I had lost contact with him myself at the beginning of June 1945, because his army unit was redeployed. My early attempts to get in touch with him again failed because of Soviet restrictions, as I later found out. Ever since I'd moved to England, my memories of him had faded into the background.

Dr Temo Melikidse as an officer in 1945.

One summer evening towards the end of the 1960s, or it may even have been in 1970, the telephone rang. It was Anneliese Friedrichs from Stralsund. Ours was almost a lifelong friendship, and I had sometimes stayed with her on my visits to East Germany. Sadly she passed away some years ago.

I still remember exactly what she said that evening, when she rang me up. I was alone at home, shelling peas.

"Are you sitting down, Gisela?" she asked me.

"No," I replied, "I'm standing at the phone."

"Then you should sit down at once, I've got to tell you something! Guess who's here with me – it's the Georgian doctor, Temo Melikidse!" her voice rang out from the telephone.

I couldn't believe it; it was impossible.

"You can speak to him," Anneliese said, "Here he is."

I was taken completely by surprise. I heard her pass the receiver to him, and then, some twenty-five years after I had last heard it, I heard the voice of the doctor who – in another time all together, in completely different circumstances – had played such a huge role in my life. Quite what we said to one another I have forgotten now, such was my nervousness and excitement.

"We'll see each other again, we'll see each other again!" That's all I can remember of what he said to me.

I learnt that he could only tarry a little while at Anneliese's. He left behind a letter, which she sent on to me. I was, though, completely bewildered after our conversation on the phone. I was widowed and, though nobody would have said anything against it if I had begun a new relationship, I never had any desire to marry again. I sensed, however, that Temo Melikidse – who had obviously learnt from Anneliese that my husband was no longer alive – wanted more than to speak to me on the telephone. I wanted to know what exactly, though I didn't want to get my hopes up.

A few days later, the letter arrived. He wrote that he wanted to see me again, that he would move heaven and earth to do so. Such an endeavour was, however, given the political circumstances – in short, the confrontational set-up between two world powers – not quite so easy to carry out. He was in the East, and I was in the West. I knew what I was letting myself in for, though. I would take no extraordinary risks, nor let my relationship with my children be harmed.

Temo Melikidse later told me exactly how he had tracked me down. After the war, he was employed by the Soviet airline Aeroflot, as the doctor responsible for the care of the employees. He lived in Tbilisi, the Georgian capital. Working for Aeroflot meant that he was able to move around quite freely, so to speak, for his own leisure, but also to find out what was happening in East Germany through friends and acquaintances. In so-called Stalinist Russia, which it became immediately following the war until 1953, it wasn't possible for him to contact anybody living abroad. Surveillance was too intensive —and the punishments draconian. Afterwards, though, it was easier. He told me that my attempts to contact him by letter between 1946 and 1949 had reached him, but such contact was forbidden by the regime so he was not able to reply.

Coincidence came to his aid once again, because Aeroflot worked together with the East German airline Interflug, as all the planes were built in the Soviet Union. Temo always asked his German colleagues, who had been trained or who had worked in the USSR, where they were from. And one day, it so happened that he met Siegfried Marquardt from Stralsund. He immediately asked Siegfried about Gisela Schönow, and Frieda and Hermann Kühn from Langenstrasse. Siegfried replied that his parents lived on that very same street. He himself lived with his family on Fährhofstrasse. When he next went back to Stralsund, this Siegfried Marquardt asked his parents about Mr and Mrs Kühn and Gisela Schönow. Yes, they knew them. They in turn asked the owners of the house, for Frieda and Hermann Kühn no longer lived there, but in a care home in Stralsund. But, with that, they were on to something. The landlady of the house, Frau Busch, knew me from the old days and knew that I was living somewhere in England.

"If you want to know more about Frau Schönow," she said, "You'd best go to the leather and toy shop at 75 Heilgeist Str and speak to Fräulein Friedrichs." And of course here Siegfried found out everything he needed to know, and he passed on the information to Temo when he returned to the Soviet Union. That is how Temo Melikidse managed to find out my whereabouts – now he knew that I lived in Wadebridge, was widowed, and had two children. As well as that, he knew my friend Anneliese in Stralsund, who was a source of further information and through whom he could establish contact with me. And so it all fell into place. Through Anneliese, we arranged our meeting.

Thus we came to meet in Stralsund in 1974, twenty-nine years after the fateful events in Niepars in 1945. I merely needed to make an application to enter East Germany, as I had done many times before. As always, it was a long, drawn-out process, but I was used to it. I needed the invitation of one person I wished to visit. I suppose that this information was important to the secret police, so that they could keep tabs on me.

For Temo, however, the journey was rather more difficult. He had a goddaughter whose mother, Nina, was Russian and father, Dieter Schertler, was East German. At some point, this family moved to Döbeln, a small town near Leipzig in the East. Temo knew both of the parents from the Soviet Union, as they had both previously lived there. Using his guardianship of the girl, Shanna, Temo had managed to secure a travel permit to visit the family. If it hadn't been for that, it would not have been possible for him to enter East Germany so easily. Temo had later led me to believe that he had good friends in the KGB, the Soviet secret service, who would leave both him and me well alone. Now that was all well and good, and at first it made me feel safe, but could I really believe it?

On 16th September 1974, Temo took the train to Stralsund, travelling like a conspirator; he wasn't actually allowed to be going to Stralsund at all, given that he had told the authorities he was going to Döbeln. But he did it anyway. I knew what time he was supposed to be arriving at Stralsund station, it was during the night. I was shaken by indescribable feelings. The images of 1945 danced before my eyes. Anneliese and I went to the station and waited for him together on the platform. When the train stopped and many people bustled around on the platform, I saw him standing to one side of the crowd. He was wearing a hat, and in his hand he had a bouquet of red roses. I recognised him immediately, and he must have recognised me again too. We stood opposite one another and he hugged me. It was completely incomprehensible to me, unsettling. I had never had serious intentions but in spite of that I found him interesting now that I saw him again. His feelings towards me were quite obvious. We stayed for around a week in Stralsund and saw each other every day. We did, though, stay with separate friends and relatives.

In the following years up until the start of the 1990s, we met up frequently. Sometimes in Dresden, sometimes in Stralsund. I often stayed with my friend Annelies Stübner, as I have already said, in the small village of Röhrsdorf near Dresden. In spite of this length of time, I was never quite sure whether his interest in me was genuine, or whether it was also the interest of the secret services. In any case, his evident closeness to the KGB indicated that it was something more. And my instincts were to be proved right. Regardless of that, though, seeing Temo again always moved me, and I always found his charm and the way he understood me very flattering.

With Temo Melikidse in Dresden.

Towards the end of the 70's I was visiting Annelies and her husband Martin Stübner in Rohrsdorf near Dresden so I could meet Temo again. It was at this time, through Temo, we met a man who worked in the research department of the Rossendorf nuclear power plant near Dresden. His name, I believe, was Waldemar Neubert. He was married to a Russian woman, Lucia, and was himself a high-ranking nuclear physicist in East Germany. Temo led me to believe that he knew him from the Soviet Union. We met up a couple of times and went on outings together, and then Waldemar Neubert made a request which surprised me. He asked me to translate an English document about nuclear facilities from the English into German. I was shocked, but did it anyway. I needed three days for the job. Temo didn't complain, although it meant that our time together was now lost. I was probably too naïve to realise that the interests of the Eastern Bloc could have been concealed behind all this.

What Temo really wanted, as he had said to me so often, was for me to go with him to Georgia. He would never have any interest in another woman, he assured me. He promised me a life of happiness, as he put it. He was chivalrous, kind, and charming towards me – I considered myself really very fortunate. His intentions were clear, but I didn't ever want to move away from the place I now called home. Our worlds were very different. Besides, I still felt the fear of 1945 in my bones. I didn't like to trust the powers of the Eastern Bloc – in many respects, the Stasi were more feared than the Soviet KGB. And the potential to cause any sort of discord between me and my children would be completely out of the question.

After November 9th 1989, when the Berlin Wall fell and the border between East and West finally crumbled, Temo would have easily been able to come to Cornwall, but I didn't want him to and couldn't allow it. I had to make that clear to him. In the end, it must have been apparent that we could not be together, because of the life I had made for myself and my children. My refusal was a huge disappointment to him – which I realised. But I had never given him false hope, even though we went through what happened in 1945 together, and even though I had got involved again by meeting him. His mistake was that he expected me to be grateful, although at the time, in 1945, I would rather have died than feel any gratitude towards him for saving my life. I know this seems harsh today.

I got the impression that some of my friends in East Germany didn't quite understand my way of thinking. They would rather that the story had a happy ending. But how could they understand when they knew nothing of my life in England?

Around Easter 1990, Peter, my elder son, travelled with the pupils from his school in Switzerland to the Soviet Union, visiting St Petersburg and Moscow. I had told Temo about this, and so he arranged to meet Peter in Moscow, at the USSR's first Macdonald's. Peter's impression confirmed what I had thought. Temo was a nice man, but, with the world how it was at the time, it was difficult to imagine a life together with our values and outlook.

Incidentally, I hadn't told my children a lot about Temo up until that point. In that sense, my journeys to the East were quite secretive at that time. In October 1990, I saw him in Dresden for the last time. Only then did I find the strength to bring an end to our contact, though without saying it so explicitly. I drew myself back from him. In my memories, though, he still has a special place. I learned later that he died in Tbilisi in around 2010.

We had thought from the start that the secret services of both the East and the West were lurking in the wings. I had long suspected that my letters from Temo and others in East Germany were being monitored. But it became apparent when, one day, a secret service agent from London appeared on my doorstep, wanting to speak to me. I let him in, but, when he told me why they had wanted to meet me, I had to refuse; their plan was that I should get involved with Temo and go to the Soviet Union as a spy. That was completely and utterly out of the question, and our talk very quickly came to a close. But the details that the man could produce about me and Temo were certainly impressive. Then he gave me a telephone number, which I was to call if I needed to. I still have his name and number – though I've never used it. Whichever service it was, MI5 or MI6, I forget, made one more attempt to recruit me. This time Peter was at home and remembers meeting the gentleman. With no warning, the doorbell rang and the same person was there. Again the visit was polite but brief. After this I never heard from them again.

I still find it difficult to understand quite why I always kept my distance from Temo. On the one hand, he saved my life at the end of the war, even though I hadn't wanted him to. In spite of that, I'm still alive now because of what he did. In the years that followed 1945, he was a constant in my, at times, lonely life. At the time, we had both been young people who were interested in each other. Nevertheless, I had considerable reservations about people from the Soviet Union. That came no doubt from the German propaganda and my own experiences at the end of the war. And after 1975, when we met up in East Germany, that was a question of my own curiosity - of course I wanted to know about what had happened to him, perhaps to test my own prejudices about the East. But a happy ending with Temo wasn't possible, as far as I was concerned, and that was for the best.

Dr Temo Melikidse.
(I never really knew his status within the Russian hierarchy but he always said he had good friends in the KGB. His collection of medals and the interest of the British Secret Service would imply he was a man of some stature.)

Friendships – Firm and Fleeting

Whilst it is true I have had some hard times in my life, I have also been blessed with some wonderful friendships that have meant so much to me and helped me through dark days. Life has taught me to treasure them.

We were a wonderful group of about 30 school friends who all used to stay in touch and many years ago I was able to attend two or three re-unions in Stralsund. Perhaps the hardships of war drew us closer together as a group; there was a real need for solidarity. In particular I must mention by name Hanni Kuchnowski and Inge Krempin. One could not have better friends. Also Anneliese Friedrichs who had the leather shop in Heilgeist Strasse. She was my constant source of information about my hometown. We have spent hours and hours on the telephone over the years.

Firm Friends. From Left: Gretel Herzig, Me, Inge Krempin, Anneliese Friedrichs, Hanni Kuchnowski.

Throughout my life, I have also had chance encounters with many people. If friendships could develop from them, I always felt that my life was enriched in some way. I found it easy to cultivate friendships and would always try to make new friends, and I have always had a need to understand and listen to people, regardless of my own situation. That is true for people living in Germany, as well as those who I got to know in England or beyond. It has always been a joy to meet new contacts in person - In short, it was my curiosity that led the way.

I can't count the visits, the journeys, the thousands of letters and cards which have cultivated and maintained these friendships – I don't even want to try! My boys still joke about the countless hours I have spent in front of my little typewriter. These ties were, to me, always worth keeping. I can also say that it has done me good, in my darkest hours, to have had understanding people at my side, even if they were not always physically present. Sadly, today many of these people are no longer with us.

Of the many people I have maintained contact with over these long years – no, decades – there are a special few who stand out. From Hamilton's family, it was his cousin Nesta and her husband Frank. They ran a plumbing business in Wadebridge. As long as I knew them, they always stood by me and gave me help and advice. Nesta leapt in to help during my absence from the shop, especially after Hamilton died. Whether it was because I was sick or because I was away on a trip, Nesta was always there. They always took the boys, too, when I had to be in the shop during school holidays.

I also want to mention the Wadebridge community especially at the time of Hamilton's death. I cannot mention them all, but those reading this will remember. So many people from this small town were simply wonderful. Local farmers who took the boys in when I was in the shop. Business people who went out of their way to help me as I was thrust unwillingly, at first, into their world. So many people gave so much help. Thank you all. It was another example of kindness to me in England and why I love Cornwall so much.

Two other, almost lifelong connections concern German women, who I met early on in my life. Our lives intersect one another like crossed lines.

The first is Annelies Stübner from Olbersdorf – I've already mentioned her. We met in 1941 during our Pflichtjahr, our compulsory year of service at the Von Hennigs' manor in Techlin,

Pomerania. We got on very well together from the moment we met, which was a good job as we lived together for a year, both far from home, and could spend our free time together. Later, as we went our separate ways again, we regularly wrote letters and cards to each other. The end of the war temporarily put a stop to our contact. But Annelies made contact again, searching for me and finding me again in Stralsund. That gave me security, back then, and confirmed the friendship's value. She was, as one might say, a good laugh, always cracking jokes and an extraordinarily friendly host. That was apparent to me during my visits to her house. She invited me to her wedding, and in January 1951 I made the journey there. Later, when I lived in England, we took up our correspondence again and it became all-encompassing. In those years, during which I visited East Germany almost every other year, I often stayed with her. In the meantime, she had moved with her husband and their two children to Röhrsdorf, a small town not far from Dresden in Saxony, near the border with what is now the Czech Republic. She worked there as a cook in a school kitchen. I knew that she was hardworking and that she knew her handicraft well. We were constantly swapping stories, whether it was in person, during visits, or by letter. Now we have both become old women, and she lives with her son near Magdeburg in Saxony-Anhalt, between Berlin and Hanover, because she cannot manage on her own. It's similar for me here in Wadebridge. My children and hers stay in touch with each other too, and have got to know each other. In May 2012, we travelled to Stralsund once more and we had our last meeting in person to date. We revelled in tales of 'the old times', happy to see each other again. We used Stralsund as our base from which to visit Techlin, where we had worked back in 1941. This more than seventy-year-long friendship, lasting no matter what happened, was always a stable, living thing of its own.

The second German woman I'd like to talk about was Ursula Schacht, known as Uschi, with whom I had been at school in Stralsund. This relationship was more complicated, and not comparable to my friendship with Annelies. I don't want to call this a friendship, but in spite of that it had a direct influence upon both of our lives. I have already told you that Uschi came to Wadebridge at Hamilton's request. At the time, I wanted to do both of them a favour – Hamilton needed help with the business and at home, and Uschi wanted to get out of East Germany.

Our fates were certainly intertwined with one another in the moment that she arrived at Hamilton's home, Toll-Gate, to become his housekeeper. That is when she realised that it was me to whom Hamilton devoted himself, and not her, as she had hoped. She saw in me a competitor. I've already mentioned that, when this crisis reached its peak, she made an attempt on her own life. In a letter which she wrote to me since, and to which I did not reply, she referred to her sole regret about her fate, which was that I had arranged for her to leave Stralsund and come to Wadebridge. I still have the letter. She blamed me for her unhappiness. We could not live under the same roof, and my relationship with Uschi seemed to be over. Hamilton found her a job working for a Jewish woman in London, who was looking for a ladies' companion. Uschi complied, because this arrangement was obviously more in keeping with her expectations and inclinations. And so she slipped away, at least for a time, out of my sight.

As I later learned, in London she got to know a man, whom she married after a while. This man came from Wellingborough, Northamptonshire, and worked at a local gasworks. He was an eligible bachelor, with his own house, a car and so on. But her relationship with her husband did not run smoothly. Uschi was always looking for something better. A man who ran a second-hand bookshop caught her eye. They began an affair, and Uschi moved after a while into his house. But this relationship came to an end when her lover was suddenly afflicted with tuberculosis and was taken to hospital. Uschi returned repentant to her husband – for she was still married to him. He took her back, and now they lived together again.

One day, it must have been in the summer of 1965, Uschi and her husband appeared in my shop in Wadebridge. She had heard of Hamilton's death through mutual contacts in Stralsund. She came up to me.

"Gila, don't you want to be friends again?" she said insistently, "How are you?"

They were staying at a bed and breakfast in Trevone, around two miles west of Padstow, and had wanted to visit me one day. I was confused – fourteen years had passed since we had last set eyes on each other, and a lot had changed. But she was asking for my forgiveness for what she had done all those years ago and I didn't want to resist it. And so we were in touch once more.

Uschi invited me to come to Wellingborough at some point. I went to see her and came upon a very beautiful house. Her husband was a kindly character. Unfortunately they had no children. Soon after I arrived back in Wadebridge her husband died.

Some time passed and, unbeknown to me, Uschi moved back to Wadebridge and married again. She became friendly with another German friend of mine, Ursel Sultemeyer, who lived nearby, and gave her own version of what had happened with Hamilton at Toll-Gate. This strained my relationship with Ursel, so I kept my distance from them both.

But then suddenly Uschi started to try and contact me again. Ursel Sultemeyer had died, and she wanted another friend.

"Sorry, I know I've made a mistake – can't we be friends again?"

This time, however, I refused. I had had enough of her dishonest so-called friendship.

We each went our separate ways, until one day I got a telephone call from her neighbour – Uschi had suffered an epileptic fit, and had been taken to hospital. The neighbour knew that I knew her. When Uschi was discharged, she came to me again to ask forgiveness. But I knew her just too well, and so I didn't get involved. Nevertheless, the fact remained that we both came from Stralsund, and so we would continue to have a connection. Our paths in life had already crossed several times.

In her last years, Uschi was somewhat less agitated. She died seven years after her second husband, Roy Jallands, in 2011. Though we stayed in touch, it was not a real friendship. But we did have a particular bond, shaped by parallel journeys through life but also by her antagonism. She spent her last days in a care home simply because she had no relatives who could care for her. I visited her there and, in a touching moment of nostalgia, she gave me her ring. It was from a jeweller in Stralsund, Stabenow – she had it made on a visit there in 2001. It carried the motif of the famous

Viking jewellery found on the island of Hiddensee – known as the Hiddensee treasure, the Viking hoard was discovered there in 1873.

Uschi's ring bearing the same motif as that of the Hiddensee treasure.

I think that, her whole life, Uschi had been broken inside. I've not been able to fathom why. She liked to play a game that was not real life. On the one hand, she had remained very affectionate, in spite of the quarrelling, but I had my reservations about our relationship. It lasted seventy-five years, though, in any case. My boys bought the empty house in Egloshayle village that had once belonged to her. And so we still have something to remind us of Uschi.

Somebody who had quite a different, though a very special meaning in my life was Ruth Udy, who, right from when I first knew her, had wanted to get married. Shortly afterwards, she became the wife of a Mr Mitchell. I have already said a little about her, because she was the housekeeper at Hamilton's house when we met. She was immediately kind to me, friendly and approachable. That was something that I very much appreciated, as a German woman in England, and so I adopted some familiar practices from her. She taught me to make Cornish pasties and yeast and saffron buns for example. I was very grateful to her for helping me to settle in. In the years when our children were growing up, we both helped each other out frequently. If I was away travelling to Germany, or to other places in Europe, Ruth would have Peter or then Bruce to stay with her. The arrangement was reciprocated, and we often had her children stay at our house as well. When we lost Hamilton, she was at my side. I can honestly say that, without Ruth, I would not have been able to weather the difficulties I came up against. Once our children had left home, we met up regularly. Her warmth and reliability throughout all those years always made me feel like I belonged. Now unfortunately, though admittedly she was a great age, she has passed away. I am happy to have known her, though, and I think about her often and with great fondness. I always picture us sitting together, drinking tea and putting the world to rights.

The World is Changing

Through my constant contact with the people I loved in my homeland, and travels to visit them in both Eastern and Western Germany, I could follow everything that happened in both places as they drifted apart over the years. In the West, wealth and freedom of thought and of trade, like in the United Kingdom, became the basis of people's lives. In the East, however, economic stagnation and paternalism ruled, as the state limited its people's freedom, ostensibly for their own good. It was painful to witness the perfidious and crude ways in which the Communist powers would use hatred, violence, lies, and fear against their own people. Although my homeland stayed in my heart my whole life, I had not wanted to live like that. I knew that the people who had been born in the East had not sought this either. Many of the people I visited wished to have the same freedom that I demonstrated with my travels and my stories. It always pained me to see that the people felt incarcerated, that they complied powerlessly. Those who wanted to leave the country put themselves in grave danger.

I remember very clearly the many times I crossed the border on my journeys from West to East Germany – it was immediately obvious on every occasion exactly how the authorities policed the border. Anybody travelling from West to East had to endure fear and intimidation in order to reach their destination.

Thinking of the people I knew and loved, I met the political developments which occurred between the East and West at the end of the 1980s with great excitement. Was this a turning point, after so many years of separation and alienation?

Yes – what had been unthinkable only a short while ago became reality in 1989. The Iron Curtain, as we called it in the West, dividing the two parts of Germany and the opposing world powers, collapsed. And with it collapsed too all of the limits and restrictions placed on the people of East Germany. Shortly before the Wall itself fell, people had filled the streets – and now they had achieved their aim. I could immediately sense that my friends and relatives were thrilled to have gained their freedom and all the opportunities that came with it. It wasn't the case for everybody, of course, but for most people. Each side had lived in constant fear of military attack by the other – though that threat was now defunct, its importance couldn't be underestimated. But of course there were worries too, and new fears. True reunification was clearly going to take considerable time.

Later I visited Stralsund, and was pleased to see how the town's streets and houses, its shops and its people, had all returned to their old ways, to how I recognised them from my youth. The all-encompassing grey gave way to radiant colours. And suddenly we could talk about all of the things that, under the old regime, had been forbidden.

Colours of Stralsund, The Old Market Square, 2016.

The people needed time to process the past. And so a chronicle appeared in my hometown of Niepars – it told the story of the years immediately following the war. My family's fate was mentioned within it. Some while later, I began to talk regularly on the telephone to this chronicle's author, Erika Meier, a former Mayor of Niepars. It was an unbelievably wonderful feeling to know the truth about my old homeland. In 2012, I went with both of my sons back to

Niepars, to the place where those tragic events had taken place in 1945. These were moments of deep reflection.

A re-developed Ossenreyer Street, the main shopping street, finally completed 70 years after the bombing.

If, in the time of the Iron Curtain, my only visitors from East Germany to Cornwall had been a few pensioners, then from 1990 onwards the younger people came too. I could show them my beautiful Cornwall. Whereas the border between East and West had made contact with my loved ones difficult, from then on everything became completely normal.

My return in 2012 to the house in Niepars where my tragedy unfolded.

The political and social developments meant that my friends and relations in my old home were brought closer to me, as though none of this had happened. We were able to telephone one another whenever we wanted, and later even to use the internet to communicate. We swapped our daily worries and joys without any obstruction. Travelling, which I had done so often, became substantially easier. We could arrange to visit each other whenever and however we pleased. I had longed for this for so many years.

Give It Time

When I had passed my seventieth year, I could no longer overlook the fact that I was growing weaker. Since the 1970s, I had suffered several problems with my knees. My doctor tried keyhole surgery in each knee to ease the problems, with each operation a few years apart. My condition only really improved for a short time, and my knees remained a problem. In 2001 and 2003, I had the difficult operations of two knee replacements. But quite apart from that, I must say I was only able to manage Hamilton House and Hamilton Court because of significant help from others and by cutting back the amount I did. It was clear to me that Peter and Bruce would have to take on these responsibilities. Thankfully, in their own time and for their own reasons, they both decided to return home and to involve themselves in the business of Hamilton House.

Peter came back first, in 1998. He gave up his job in Switzerland to do so, and he started something new back in England – he was now a qualified sports therapist and opened a small practice in Hamilton Court, where we built an extra room above the garage. At the same time, he worked on the medical side with some rugby teams and individual athletes at competitions. Indeed he was part of the sports massage team at the Sydney Olympics in 2000, when again he was able to spend time with Bruce. This type of work left him with enough time to take care of the matters relating to our properties. As well as that, he still took part in sport himself, particularly cycling. He would meet up with friends in Switzerland at least once a year to go cycling or skiing.

As time progressed and my age increased, he had to look after me too. I can still manage things around the house, but in the last two or three years I've not been able to do things outside without help from Peter or Bruce. I'm very grateful to both of them for being there for me and for their support. Because of that, I can have a life which is as active as possible.

Bruce came back in July 2003. He found a job here, through an old friend who was a John Deere dealer in Devon. He works there three days a week.

His job provides additional income, but also maintains an interest in the industry he made his career. He kept his house in Melbourne and rented it out, probably in the assumption that he might use it again one day. He'll have to make that decision for himself. I take particular joy in his part within a male voice choir, a very prestigious one in Cornwall. It is the Loveny Male Voice Choir, which is based in the artistic village of St Neot. The choir practises there once a week and gives concerts many times during the year across Cornwall and beyond.

He has also been a part of the Trelawny Male Choir, some seventy to eighty voices strong, which has toured both the west and east coasts of Canada. A particular highlight was a performance of massed male Cornish choirs at London's Royal Albert Hall in November 2013, some six hundred voices strong. Although I could not attend, friends from Germany, including my godson Ingo, travelled to London to listen. They greatly enjoyed it. If performances are local, Peter and I go to listen too.

That is how the years have elapsed. When I handed over all of the business matters to my sons, I was able to spend more time with my friends who were still alive – visits to and from Wadebridge, letters and telephone calls with relatives and friends in Germany. Sadly there are fewer and fewer as time goes on. Loneliness does creep up on you, though I managed to make the journey to Stralsund in 2012, perhaps for the last time. Peter and Bruce accompanied me. It was a delight to catch up with so many old friends. But even when I'm away from Stralsund, my particular interest in this place is not lost. With today's means of communication, together with the support of my two sons, I can keep up with current events, so that I feel as though I'm part of what is going on. It's always particularly pleasing when relatives of mine visit from Stralsund, bringing local delicacies with them.

In the last five or six years, Peter and Bruce have planned and carried out the renovations of Hamilton House together. That was once again a joint effort. Over the course of time, through general wear and tear, the building had deteriorated and fallen behind modern standards. This all had to be fixed so that Hamilton's business, his legacy, was secured for his sons. I'm happy that they've managed it. I think it is in keeping with Hamilton's ways.

Renovated Hamilton House in 2016.

Now all that remains is to look after a successful, fruitful business. Peter and Bruce take care of its management together. At the same time, I can look back on what I have done for Hamilton's legacy and be reassured that it was worthwhile. It was hard work, certainly, but it was successful in the end. Now it is ready to pass on to the next generation.

Insight

Now, having discussed my entire life, its most important events and people, I am both relieved and satisfied. In times past I have sometimes talked openly about various people and pieces of my life. That was important to me, but I have never spoken about my whole life completely, and in such detail. The diary I started so long ago has unfortunately remained incomplete, although I do look things up if I remember something. It should tell the story of my whole life, but I've not managed that, for several reasons. That is why I am pleased to have recorded my memories and to have kept photos and documents together in this way.

The diary entry for 29th January 1951, the day I departed Stralsund to begin my journey to Wadebridge, marks one of the most important turning points in my life. The deaths of my whole family at the end of the war had changed my existence immediately – I could not have predicted the events of 1st May 1945, nor was I prepared for them – and afterwards I was often plagued by doubt as to how and where I ought to live my life; at times even considering suicide out of acute despair. These traumatising moments determined from then on the course of my life. I surrendered myself again to the daily grind, not having any long-term goals, but it always felt as though I were being pushed by somebody. I described that need to go on in my diary, with a verse by Goethe:

Das Muss ist hart, aber beim Muss kann der Mensch allein zeigen, wie's inwendig mit ihm steht! Willkürlich leben, kann jeder.

'Must' is a hard word, but only in dealing with this 'must' can one show what one is made of. Anyone can live arbitrarily.

I'd like to recite here my diary entry for 29th January 1951, as it shows that need propelling me to move forward.

> *Today I must once again look back on everything. I believe I'll be able to say that my journey at the beginning of September '50 was a turning point for the rest of my life.*

I made the decision to go to England. Everything was set in motion by the Caritas organisation. My journey there was authorised. My plane ticket was booked at first for 18th December, and then for 8th January 1951. Now it will really happen on 19th February. On the one hand, I'm very excited, but I found it so very difficult to say goodbye to Aunt Frieda. She looked so forlorn. Should I stay here with her instead? Put away the longing to travel that I have never felt before? I feel that I must go. These are the two sides which divide me, pulling me one way and then the other, hour after hour, day after day. Won't somebody tell me what I should do? But most children leave their parents' house when they've grown up. Am I making a mistake, leaving Aunt Frieda alone? Will I hate myself if I go? If only God would show me which path I should take. And I still hope that, in two years' time when I come back, I will see Aunt Frieda again. She has to go on living for me. She'll see me happy yet. Let the Lord satisfy my wishes and give me peace at last...

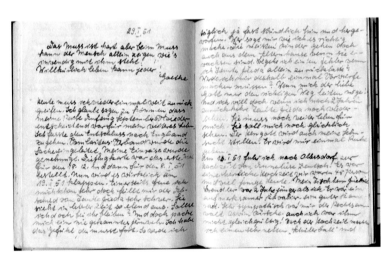

Pages from my diary.

Back then I thought in fact that I would be able to return to East Germany after two years. Politically, it was an illusion, and personally, a hope. My homesickness for Stralsund and Niepars is still within me, but it is for my happy times before the events which so cruelly changed my life.   Such times are there no more. The following proverb adorns the hallway of my house in Wadebridge:

Forge your path into the distance – then take your home with you in your heart.

A proverb from home.

I feel that this proverb applies to me when I compare my home with my childhood and my youth before 1st May 1945.

A stronger, more intense feeling is that my homesickness is my guilt, which I carry around with me. I have talked about it already. I brought back the poison which killed my family – that weighs heavily on my soul. I ask myself again and again whether it was better for them to have drunk the poison than to be subjected to some unspecified sort of violence or another, worse torture. The thought will not leave me that my life and how it played out might have been a punishment from God for this supposed guilt. Nobody could, nor can they now, take this guilt from me, how could they? The images of their deaths are burnt into my memory. They surface again without warning almost every night. The doubt will stay inside me until my last breath.

Living with this burden has shaped me in a particular way. I have had to bear it for all this time. I think that the strength it has taken to get me here comes from my parents. I, hope that my boys and the people closest to me will never have to live through such experiences, but I hope that they still possess this inner strength to conquer evil. It fills me with great worry even today that, in spite of the painful, distressing experiences of my generation, the wars and murders in the world might not stop.

Naturally over the course of my life I have made some mistakes – that goes without saying. If I cannot correct them, at least I have been forgiven for them, and I have learnt from them. The things I have been able to achieve during my life fill me with happiness and satisfaction; they are my reward. What I have gained does not quite balance what I have lost, however, because everything that stands on the 'lost' side weighs heavily on my mind, for I still feel each loss keenly. As a consequence, sadness resonates through my reflection on my life. But, with all my strength and my entire will, I have managed to do what I thought I could. In that sense, I can spend my remaining days and years here in Wadebridge with my little bit of happiness and peace.

A view over Wadebridge, Cornwall, from the River Camel towards the western side of the town.

Epilogue

For as long as I can remember Gisela Hawkey has always been a special person for me. From my early childhood she was close to my thoughts, but far away and unreachable. This was a contradiction. Gisela was my Godmother, but living far away in the West of England. Throughout my life I have been interested in her story. In my early years, like me, she was living in Stralsund, later moving to Wadebridge, in Cornwall, England. Over time, from my family, I have heard pieces of her story.

Her past was in our hometown Stralsund, but there was also a new life with her husband, Hamilton, in Cornwall. Her early visits to Stralsund in the 1950's I still remember. She spoke of a life so very different from that which I knew inside the GDR (German Democratic Republic or East Germany). From the time I heard these early stories Wadebridge, Cornwall was only a small spot on the map, but I felt a strong connection that still exists today.

Later as an adult I always felt Gisela's address, and her stories, were directing my life. My own decision to leave the GDR was influenced by the contacts I had on the west side of the Iron Curtain. In looking back these influences were good for me.

In the past 8 years I have often visited Gisela. I wanted to know more about her life, and the life in Cornwall. I was thankful for this long held connection. We got to know each other better and spoke a lot about our early lives. Step by step I understood the highs and lows of her life. I was amazed by the strength she had shown throughout her life given the obstacles and tragedies she had experienced.

In 2012 I retired and I invited Gisela to Stralsund as I knew she was still homesick for her home town. She longed to travel once more to Stralsund. Peter and Bruce were also able to travel and visit the town with her. During this time I had the opportunity to ask if I could write her story. She readily agreed and I was happy and grateful to think I could document this remarkable story. We worked for approximately one year to write the story. Over a period of 2 weeks, in Cornwall, I sat with Gisela every day and recorded her words on my computer to later put into text. At times the work released strong memories and produced intense feelings and we formed a special bond. I'm thankful to Gisela and her sons for trusting me to write her story.

It is a story that deserves to be told.

Ingo Küster.